What are leaders in Christian ministry, sports, and business saying about *Bottom-Line Faith?*

"It's one thing to talk about commitment, but it's quite another to demonstrate it. What characteristics reveal a person's serious commitment to Jesus Christ? Larry Kreider's *Bottom-Line Faith* masterfully answers that key question. Through crisp, clear examples of people who paid the price to 'walk the talk' of being a follower of Jesus Christ, Kreider shows us what it means to be an authentic Christian. This book will become a manual for believers who are serious about mirroring Jesus Christ in and through their lives."

Rod Cooper, Ph.D.
National Director of Educational Ministries, Promise Keepers
Author of *We Stand Together: Men of Color and Reconciliation*

"*Bottom-Line Faith* is the right title for this very helpful, from-the-shoulder book. Larry Kreider is a trustworthy, credible evangelist and disciple. He actually *does* the things he writes about. This is the reason this book feels authentic. While all Christians will find this book to be helpful, I especially recommend it to men. Kreider thinks in a male way in a world that needs a compassionate, reflective, straightforward message to men. I like the biblical foundation of *Bottom-Line Faith* because the Bible is really the bottom line of all Christian writing."

Jay Kesler
President, Taylor University
Author of *Restoring a Loving Marriage*

"For a long time we have needed a good manual to help people understand the basics of their faith. I think Larry Kreider's book does just that. He has taken the critical elements of a good foundation and explains them in a way that a twenty-first-century man or woman can understand. Thanks, Larry, for this important contribution to ministry."

Roger Cross
President, Youth for Christ/USA

"With many fascinating stories and great skill, Larry Kreider puts *commitment* in plain language and practical contexts. He helps us see how moment-by-moment living for Christ and trusting in him can be an exciting adventure. I recommend this inspiring and motivational book for individual or group study."

Steve Douglass
Executive Vice President, Campus Crusade for Christ
Author of *Enjoying Your Walk with God*

D1021706

"The fertile mind and caring heart of Larry Kreider are revealed in this challenging and practical book. Filled with insight and inspiration, *Bottom-Line Faith* will stretch your walk with the Savior. This promises to be just the first of masterful offerings from the pen of Larry Kreider."

John F. Tolson, D. Min.
Founder, Chairman of the Board, The Gathering/USA, Inc.
Founder, National Basketball Association Chapel Program

"Read Larry Kreider's book. The ten characteristics it describes are vital to a living, breathing, 'bottom-line faith,' and each one is richly illustrated with biblical and contemporary examples. From humility and diligence to investing in the lives of others, these traits of the Christlike person will most assuredly make a difference in individuals, families, and communities."

H. Edwin Young, D.D.
Senior Pastor, Second Baptist Church of Houston
Author of *Been There, Done That, Now What?* and *Romancing the Home*

"Larry Kreider has a robust and exuberant faith—a faith big enough to lift the spirit of anyone whose life comes into contact with his, a faith tough enough to bend without breaking under the pressures of living in this sin-sick, sorrow-torn world, and a faith wide enough to embrace not only his own neighborhood but also the whole earth. Bottom line? Get his book, read it, learn from it, and apply it to your own life's journey. It will make a difference—and then so will you!" **J. Howard Edington, D.D.**
Senior Minister, First Presbyterian Church, Orlando

"This book is must reading for anyone who considers himself or herself to be a Christian. As I read *Bottom-Line Faith*, Larry Kreider challenged me, stirred me, and encouraged me to become a more committed follower of Jesus Christ. Anyone who reads this book will be humbled, inspired, and changed." **Adolph Coors**
Founder, Adolph Coors IV Evangelistic Association

"I've known Larry Kreider for many years. His book *Bottom-Line Faith* captures Larry at his best: helping people make their faith practical and applicable. This is a good book for discovering whether your spiritual life is a slam dunk or an air ball. I will be recommending *Bottom-Line Faith* to many people. It's a winner, just like Larry Kreider." **Pat Williams**
General Manager, Orlando Magic

"Whether in my career as a pro golfer or in the ongoing struggles of life, I want to know the bottom line of what it means to be a committed Christian. Now I know—and so will countless others who read this book."

Paul Azinger
Winner of the 1993 PGA Championship
Co-author of *Zinger*

"*Bottom-Line Faith* takes us through practical applications of our faith. For those of us who continually struggle to take Christianity into our marketplace, the book is filled with biblical truths and references. It is unique in that it is challenging in its text and also doubles as a workbook for specific biblical reference."

C. Fred Fetterolf
Retired President and COO, Aluminum Company of America

"This book is a stirring reminder of the essentials of our faith. Through Larry Kreider's own deep and diverse life experiences, the reader is mentored into a closer walk with Christ. *Bottom-Line Faith* is a practical guide to applying our Christianity to the daily cares and joys of life. Larry gives us a fresh vision for victorious Christian living. The biblical examples and study questions challenge us to dig deeper within ourselves, to move out of our comfort zone, and to realize our potential as committed Christians."

John E. Brown III
Arkansas State Senate
Executive Director of the Windgate Charitable Foundation
Former President of John Brown University in Siloam Springs, Arkansas

"Larry Kreider's new book, *Bottom-Line Faith: Ten Characteristics of Committed Christians,* is wonderful reading. Chapter three, 'Put Others First in a "Me First" World' is exceptional. The use of inspirational true stories provides great examples for everyone."

Gary Strack
President/CEO, Orlando Regional Healthcare System

bottom-line FAITH

LARRY KREIDER
WITH TERRY WHALIN

Tyndale House Publishers, Inc.

WHEATON, ILLINOIS

Library of Congress Cataloging-in-Publication Data

Kreider, Larry.
   Bottom-line faith : ten characteristics of committed Christians /
Larry Kreider with Terry Whalin.
     p.   cm.
   Includes bibliographical references.
   ISBN 0-8423-6904-X (SC : alk. paper)
    1. Commitment to the church. I. Whalin, Terry. II. Title.
BV4520-K67   1995
248.4—dc20   95-17229

Printed in the United States of America

01 00 99 98 97 96 95
7   6   5   4   3   2   1

Dedicated to
BEAVER FURLEY
You left a legacy of faith,
though you left too soon.

CONTENTS

ACKNOWLEDGMENTS

BEHIND every project are those who encourage, co-labor, and sharpen the final product.

I am deeply grateful for the encouragement of Dr. John Tolson and the men of The Gathering. I thank my co-laborers, Terry Whalin, who helped in the final stages of writing, and Lynn Vanderzalm, my Tyndale House editor. I deeply appreciate my wife, Susan, and my administrative assistant, Anne Davis, who sharpened the final product.

INTRODUCTION

IT'S risky to declare that this book is about the ten characteristics of a committed Christian because the minute I choose a number, people begin to count. They add to the list or subtract from it based on their interpretation of which characteristics are valid or invalid.

Therefore, from the beginning, understand that the ten characteristics I include in this book aren't an exhaustive list. There may well be a hundred.

This book doesn't cover the basic assumptions about Christianity or biblical essentials, such as prayer, commitment to marriage and family, witnessing, stewardship, balanced living, or the necessity of a quiet time. Although all of these basics are critically important, they are already the topics of numerous books.

This book also does not cover specific lifestyle characteristics or moral issues such as sexual purity, stewardship, or matters of social justice. However, they eventually end up integrated into a "bigger picture."

This bigger picture can be summarized in two words: *bottom-line expectations.* Jesus asks us to join him with the statement, "Come unto me. . . ." He longs for us to reconnect ourselves and others to the ultimate Source of life and meaning in the universe—and people respond. The problem is that people often "join" Christianity without knowing the bottom-line expectations or without being committed to following through on those expectations.

So that's the purpose of this book: to show, step-by-step, how to pursue without hesitation the goal of total commitment to Christ and his work in the world. Committed followers do not seek to obtain perfection, and they don't have false expectations of what their Christian commitment will accomplish. Instead, they put on their track shoes and run to finish the race.

I can't guarantee results for pursuing these characteristics. But I *can* guarantee that without following these characteristics, nothing of lasting value will emerge from the few short years we are on this earth.

Change occurs one life at a time, one day at a time. As you consider each of the following chapters, I pray that they will help you refine your own character traits as you impact the world for Christ.

1

Yield Control—
Without Giving Up

*More basic than all other human needs is the craving to
control one's own destiny, to be free to realize one's full
potential without restraints from anyone.*

FRIEDRICH NIETZSCHE

PETER Fox came to Orlando with a goal—completing an
Arnold Palmer golf-course community in Isleworth, the
wealthy section of town. Because his dad had been president
of the Minnesota Twins for forty-six years, Peter had grown
up with a passion for sports and building things from scratch.
As a child, he had broken down a television set to see if he
could rebuild it.

When the Isleworth course was nearing completion, Peter
was approached by a business friend to develop new real-

estate projects. His responsibilities would be to concentrate on acquisitions such as a large downtown office tower, an apartment project, and a cargo facility at Orlando International Airport. Because developing projects was in his blood, Peter didn't think twice before taking this new job. It seemed perfectly suited to his abilities.

Later, Peter discovered he had jumped in too quickly. He had failed to investigate the financial health of the older real-estate projects. Unfortunately, they were in deep trouble. There wasn't enough financial muscle behind the profitable projects to keep the company afloat. Within a year and a half, three of the projects were in foreclosure. Because Peter was loyal, he worked personally and tirelessly to solve his business friend's real-estate dilemmas.

But when the financial crisis was nearly over, Peter faced some tough questions. First, was this what he wanted to do for the rest of his life? Second, in twenty years of real-estate development, why had he never asked God—or anyone else—for help or discernment?

Peter decided to join a small group study for men and began to search Scripture. In the process, he discovered that he wanted to get to know Jesus, but in so doing, he found that he didn't know himself.

Through Peter's study, he determined that he needed to turn over the reins of his life to God. Not only would the Lord be his joint partner in future business ventures, he also asked the Lord to help him use his gift of being able to develop things from scratch.

Today Peter Fox is a man on a mission. He and his partner have created several new companies, including Capital Management Corp., which owns cargo-storage facilities at the airport, and Capital Cargo Corp., an air-cargo-freight service transporting perishable goods between Orlando and Latin America.

A recipient of God's blessing, Peter discovered an important characteristic of being a committed Christian: We must let go of our control on life and hand everything over to God. This is a bottom-line expectation for those who want to follow God. Although the salvation of our souls is free, the one who purchases that salvation has a deed on everything we own, every relationship we count dear, and every dream for which we long.

Although many churches teach this yielding principle, at times the implications for daily life are diluted. Perhaps this is because yielding control—even to God—seems to contradict the "pull yourself up by your own bootstraps" mentality that is so pervasive in our society.

Yielding Control: It's Not Natural

Yielding control is not easy because it sounds like quitting or giving up. And that goes against our nature of striving, overcoming, and competing.

Everyone faces things that are out of control—a class bully, an illness, an unjust supervisor, difficulties in relationships. Let's look at how we experience this lack of control as children, through current trends in work and in marriage, and through circumstances and events of nature.

Early Lessons in Control

When we are children, we discover our lives are often beyond our control. For instance, take Luke, an energetic ten-year-old. John, his father, likes to describe his son as a "piece of work."

Luke constantly tests the waters of authority to see how much he can get away with. One day John got an urgent call to return home. The water faucet on the side of their home was spurting like Old Faithful at Yellowstone.

Luke was the culprit. Earlier he had hammered on the

spigot with some bricks until it finally broke. As much as Luke wanted to fix the faucet, he couldn't. A solid stream of water shot high over the house. In addition, Luke learned he couldn't control his mother's attitude about the faucet. He was in trouble!

It took a professional plumber (and a professional bill) to replace the five-dollar part. Luke couldn't wiggle out of his responsibility. Later that night, John talked with his son about the faucet. "It's been a difficult day, huh, Luke?"

"Yeah," Luke said, then pointed to his parents' bedroom. "But you've got to do something about that woman!"

Luke had learned that he was not in charge but answered to higher authorities—his mother and father. After parents, the next layer of authority for a child to challenge might be a schoolteacher, a coach, an older sibling, or eventually the police. Stories abound of adolescents who settle a score with a personal enemy through an act of violence. When the case goes to court, nicely groomed defendants sit stunned and often in tears when the verdict is read. These young adults are shocked at the consequences. I can't help but wonder if that was the first time someone was big and powerful enough to block their destructive behavior, to show they aren't always in control. Sadly, for many children, their "moment of truth" arrives late, and they pay the painful consequences.

Work Shifts

A revolution is occurring in our workplace: We are moving from an industrial era into an informational era. Thousands of white-collar workers are being laid off or are required to take early retirement from corporations going through major reorganization.

These corporate shifts are increasing at a rapid rate. Jim Seneff, founder and owner of CNL, Inc., the largest real-estate syndicator in the United States, calls this process "hyper change." He predicts that in the next ten years, more changes will occur in the workplace than in the history of civilization. After these changes, only one percent of the workforce will be in agriculture, 10 percent in manufacturing, and the other 89 percent in the service and information sector.

These macroeconomic shifts are beyond our control. Seneff predicts that by the year 2000, 50 percent of all workers will not work for a corporation but will be self-employed consultants or specialists working out of their homes.

Where does this leave us? While we have no control over these changes, we can make preparations to offer a necessary service in this new arena.

Sabotaged Marriages

People rarely go into a marriage intending to sabotage their relationship with their spouse. Yet approximately 25 percent of original marriages end in divorce.[1] What happened? Sometimes the expectation levels are too high.

Let's take this husband, for example. He thought he was marrying a beautiful woman with an enormous capacity for household chores, an eight-to-five job, and nightly amorous intentions. Instead he got an exhausted, cranky woman who needs daily remodeling and who doesn't appreciate being taken for granted by an underpaid, oversexed couch potato. Because his expectations far exceed reality, he may try to control his wife by verbally assaulting her or by withholding what she wants until she meets those expectations.

On the other hand, perhaps the wife was looking forward to living with a kind, understanding, hardworking man who looked for every opportunity to help around the house. She anticipated someone who would share joint responsibilities in caring for their children and who eagerly looked forward to meaningful conversations. But what she has in a marriage partner is far from her expectations.

When neither husbands nor wives realize their expectations, they often try to force the other into roles they have imagined. This may work for a while, but they can't control how the spouse will emotionally react to these attempts at manipulation. They may wake up to the fact that their spouse no longer loves them and frantically attempt to win back that love. They may read books on how to rekindle romantic flames, but nothing works. Then one day, a spouse leaves the house for the last time—and the other has no control over his or her leaving.

Circumstances of Nature

At 4:30 A.M. on January 17, 1994, an alarm woke the entire city of Los Angeles. The earth heaved and shivered like a subterranean behemoth stretching its rippling muscles and spitting fire and smoke into the predawn air. Three-story apartments were reduced to two, and sports facilities collapsed.

Television networks fed the latest tallies of death and destruction to an anxious world. ABC news anchor Peter Jennings stood with the setting sun sinking slowly over his shoulder and the dust haze still lingering noticeably on the horizon. His final comment was, "The people of Los Angeles realized they have no control over what has happened to them today."

We can't control circumstances. It's not hard to acknowledge that we can't predict if or when a fire will sweep a Chicago neighborhood or a hurricane devastate an East Coast community. We can't control whether our newborn child will be healthy or impaired, or whether an earthquake will rumble beneath our home.

Yes, we can act responsibly. We can build our homes with fire-retardant materials and construct them to meet hurricane and earthquake codes. And a mother can take care of her health during pregnancy and eliminate harmful stimulants that might threaten the unborn baby. But so much still remains out of our control.

Nancy Kerrigan's training program for the Winter Olympics in Norway was right on schedule until a second-rate thug tried to break her knee. Until that moment Kerrigan had no idea that a sinister plot existed to prevent her from participating in Lillehammer. Kerrigan could control her training regime. She could calculate the odds of being a world-class figure skater by the amount of discipline she combined with her athletic ability, but she couldn't control the envy and greedy aspirations of her competitors.

Hope for a World out of Control

The Bible says much about circumstances beyond our control. No man felt more bewildered than Job. Everything dear to him—family, health, possessions—was ripped away. As hard as Job tried, he couldn't figure out what God was doing. Out of the agony of his despair he cried out to God for answers: "Where then does wisdom come from? Where does understanding dwell? It is hidden from the eyes of every living thing, concealed even from the birds of the air" (Job 28:20-21).

At first glance, God's response seemed harsh: "Who is this that darkens my counsel with words without knowledge? Brace yourself like a man; I will question you, and you shall answer me. . . . Can you trust him to bring in your grain and gather it to your threshing floor? . . . Will the one who contends with the Almighty correct him?" (Job 38:2-3; 39:12; 40:2). Basically God told Job not only that he lacked control of life's circumstances but also that he didn't have the bigger picture in mind.

The hope that God offered Job was twofold: First, stop trying to interpret every circumstance and figure everything out; second, realize that your role is unique and important—even though you don't fully understand how this circumstance fits in the overall script for your life.

Full Steam Ahead!

When you yield control of your life to God, you still have to overcome several mind games before moving full steam ahead. The thought of yielding control conjures up mental images of people who gave total control to cult leaders like Charles Manson or David Koresh. Such people gave up their discernment, and they were led like sheep to the slaughter.

But those who come to Christ are asked to do exactly the opposite. They are asked to be "transformed by the renewing of your mind" (Romans 12:2). A godly mind is an active mind: studying, exploring, challenging, discussing, and processing all forms of information. Yielding control turns the switch of your mind on, not off. Yielding control means we focus on finding out what God has to say about every aspect of life.

Another mental image to eliminate is thinking that aggressive pursuit of goals is not scriptural. Some people feel as if they are an eight-cylinder engine revving up the r.p.m.s while in neutral. It's not the Bible that is holding them back; it's their preconceived notions that haven't allowed their lives to be put in gear. A committed Christian seeks to know the mind of God, sets his or her mind on that course, and then moves ahead with a wonderful sense of inner peace that the ultimate results have been left in the hands of God. Like Job, the committed Christian will allow God to direct the play.

When Jesus said, "I must be about my Father's business," he knew the contents of his father's business and proceeded in a resolute and focused manner (Luke 2:49, KJV). There was no sense of resignation or passivity in Jesus. Whatever yieldedness looks like, it is not some media stereotype of a directionless, lazy wallflower.

Another person who was yielded to God was the Old Testament prophet Nehemiah, who patiently waited for the doors of opportunity to open. Once they opened, Nehemiah moved full steam ahead. For seventy years the Babylonians held the

Jewish nation in captivity. Nehemiah had an influential position as the cupbearer to King Artaxerxes, but he had no control over his future, over the fate of his fellow Jewish captives, or over the physical condition of Jerusalem (which was a matter of great concern to him). As the first trickle of exiled refugees found their way back to Israel, Nehemiah began to hear about the deterioration of the walls surrounding Jerusalem. He still didn't have the power to do anything about it.

Nehemiah did what he could: He prayed. He couldn't hide his anguish over the situation in his prayers or in the presence of the king. As a faithful servant, he found favor with the king and was released to organize a workforce to rebuild the walls of Jerusalem.

Nehemiah could have served the rest of his days in the Susa palace. Instead, he took advantage of the opportunities he had. When all he could do was pray, he prayed. When he was given permission to launch a rebuilding effort, he did it. As a result the job was finished in fifty-two days! (Nehemiah 1:1–6:15).

Though it seems like a contradiction, yielding control and moving full steam ahead are not mutually exclusive. As Christians, we can make plans, set goals, fight with all our strength, and, as Churchill said, "Never give in." We can do so knowing that we can rejoice at the victories accomplished and that our failures have a purpose larger than our understanding.

Three Benefits of Yielding Control to God

The Bible is a textbook on the importance of yielding our life to God. Jesus said, "Come to me, all you who are weary and burdened, and I will give you rest" (Mathew 11:28). This century is full of exhausted and burdened people who don't want to add to those burdens by yielding control of their lives to God if there is no perceived benefit. Jesus didn't apologize for making an offer the weary find hard to refuse: "rest for your souls" (Matthew 11:29). In time, growing Christians learn that the true joy of yielding comes in the opportunities for giving, not in figuring out how their needs can be met.

God Can Be Trusted to Take Care of You

Non-Christians can't conceive of a God who is kind. They view life's tragedies as proof that nothing or no one intervenes or protects. But Jesus was emphatically clear that those who put him first in their lives would be taken care of: "Seek first his kingdom and his righteousness, and all these things [life's necessities] will be given to you as well" (Matthew 6:33).

Once people are committed to being "kingdom followers," they begin to realize that God will take care of them. Life won't be trouble-free or exempt from heartache, but it will be purposeful. God can be trusted to take care of us, regardless of the circumstances.

Everyone wants to know the purpose for things like earthquakes, hurricanes, wars, and other tragedies. But we really ought to ask the same questions when good things happen. What about a job promotion, a clean bill of health after a medical exam, or an escalating stock portfolio?

Throughout Scripture, God reveals he works by a plan. In the book of Genesis, God called a people to be his own, planned for their redemption, planned their present and future livelihood, and then planned for their growth and success as a nation. As time marches forward, he plans for their return to Jerusalem after a lengthy seventy-year period of captivity in Babylon.

When King David declared, "Many, O Lord my God, are the wonders you have done. The things you planned for us no one can recount to you; were I to speak and tell of them, they would be too many to declare" (Psalm 40:5), he didn't say everything we experience is delightful. But he assumes that

God is good and all experiences weave a tapestry that, beyond any individual dreams, is more wonderful than we could imagine. Although the back side of that tapestry reveals a tangle of gnarled knots and twisted threads, the front side ultimately will reveal how meaningful each life experience can be for those who are yielded to him.

It's God's Job to Show You His Plan

No kingdom follower is required to crack the code that reveals God's hidden plan. God wants to communicate with us. In fact, the Bible gives numerous examples of God on a search-and-find mission. In some cases, God gave detailed and direct guidance. In the book of Acts, Paul was called to specific locations through dreams, and occasionally direct verbal messages were sent.

God's creative options for communicating with us are unlimited. First and foremost, he communicates with us through the principles in Scripture. We use our mind to study and wrestle with the implications of his written Word. But we don't have to figure it out by ourselves; we have the Holy Spirit, a helper or instructor who helps us understand the meaning of the text and how to apply it to everyday situations. Even through the most remote and obscure passages, there are times when the light goes on in our head as we read verses that apply to our present situation and dilemma. At such times, decisions are no longer made in a fog but in the light God offers every person who will take the time to study diligently.

What happens when we blow it? From Scripture, it is clear that all of God's special people had flaws. But God communicated to flawed people in spite of their failures, in spite of Abraham's impatience, Moses' anger, David's lust, and Jonah's disobedience. And he will communicate with us in spite of our failures too! As our sovereign benefactor, God will not leave us impoverished or forsaken. With this firm knowledge, it is easier for us to move on, take risks, and leave anxiety behind. As one friend from Laguna Beach, California, said after hundreds of people had lost their homes and possessions in a firestorm, "Romans 8:28 did not burn."

Yielding Control Is a Productive Way to Live

It is dangerous to say that everyone who lives a yielded life will be a "productive" person, because everyone has a different interpretation of what *productive* means. A highly driven person measures productivity by measurable goals achieved. A perfectionist measures it by a flawless performance—not the number of performances. A gregarious person counts the number of loyal friends and the quantity of meaningful interactions.

When the Bible refers to productivity or fruitfulness, it is measured by God's definition and standards, which include the fruit of the Spirit: internal qualities of character and faith, such as love, joy, peace, patience, kindness, goodness, faithfulness, gentleness, and self-control (Galatians 5:22-23). God measures people from the inside, not the outside. For instance, he may allow a person to feel unproductive—unable to achieve a measurable, bottom-line goal—so that person will become fruitful in patience.

Jesus was the most productive person ever to live on earth. He was productive and fruitful because he was totally yielded to the will of his Father. None of us can perfectly follow God's design as Jesus did, but we can attempt to model his yieldedness, a major tenet of his teaching.

The analogy Christ used to describe this truth was the relationship between the branches and the vine (John 15:1-8). Every Jewish person who heard Christ speak these words understood that only the branches attached to the vine are productive. They also understood it was impossible for a branch not to bear fruit in such a condition. Therefore, Jesus' analogy emphasized not only the importance of abiding in the vine but also the ability to relax and know that life automatically flows from the vine to the branches. However, what is not guaranteed is the health of the branches; that depends on environmental conditions, such as being located high enough on the vine to receive sunlight and to be free from the dust often collected on the lower branches. When a branch does not reach its potential, the keeper of the vineyard has the obligation to prune and regraft so the harvest is as bountiful as possible.

On the human level, we produce spiritual fruit as we abide in Christ and as we yield the control of our lives to him. Every believer goes through painful experiences in order to reach his or her spiritual potential. Fruitfulness is not salesmanship; it's not marketing our spiritual gems. It's living out the life of Christ in such a way that people are attracted to the real thing. Nothing in the world can replace the effectiveness of Christians who have been wounded in the pruning process, speaking and living authentically. Although these people may not understand what is happening to them, they know they are part of a grand design. They know that God knows what he is doing.

> *How he bends but never breaks*
> *When our good he undertakes;*
> *How he uses whom he chooses*
> *And with every purpose fuses him:*
> *By every act induces him*
> *To try his splendor out—*
> *God knows what he's about!*
>
> Oswald Sanders, *Spiritual Leadership*[2]

There are some wonderful benefits that go along with abiding in Christ. Prayer becomes effective and joy overflows, resulting in increased attractiveness to others and increased productivity and fruitfulness.

Yielding—an Act of the Will

Have you yielded control of your life to God? Perhaps you've tried on several occasions, but you're not sure you know what to do. Here are three tangible suggestions to help you.

Pray

If you have never told God you've made the decision to yield your life fully to his control, do so—and phrase it in your own words. Once you have done that, understand that yielding is a daily process. Hand over the reins of your life to God every single day. When you feel anxious and you try to manipulate or control your circumstances, say, "I forgot, God. This is for you to handle, not me."

Transfer the Title of Your Concerns

Sometimes it helps to list your concerns on a sheet of paper. Then write at the bottom of the page: I hereby transfer the title for the above mentioned concerns to God.

Signed _____ Date _____

Sing a Song

Either silently in your heart or out loud in private, sing a chorus to help you emotionally release yourself to God's care. The hymn "Have Thine Own Way, Lord" may be a good place to start.

> *Have Thine own way, Lord!*
> *Have Thine own way!*
> *Thou art the Potter, I am the clay.*
> *Mold me and make me after Thy will,*
> *While I am waiting, yielded and still.*

Or you may want to sing the chorus from Kathy Troccoli's song "My Life Is in Your Hands":

My life is in your hands.
My heart is in your keeping.
I'm never without hope,
Not when my future is with you.
My life is in your hands,
And though I may not see clearly,
I will lift my voice and sing.
'Cause your love does amazing things.
Lord, I know
My life is in your hands.[3]

The Bottom Line

When you put your life and circumstances into God's hands, you will experience some great benefits:

- A new peace will flood your life. God is in charge, so you can relax.
- You can live each day with a greater sense of purpose. It's not your responsibility to guide your life and control it. You have put yourself in the hands of the Creator of the universe. He is in ultimate charge of your program. Your responsibility is to walk hand in hand with God.
- You can begin to take yourself less seriously. Lighten up! God is directing the overall plan for your life.

It takes practice for us to give up control. It's not a onetime experience but requires daily yielding. One day you will yield your worries about your children to God. Another day you will yield a work experience. Yet another day you will yield other relationships. The world will continue to rush about

15

frantically, striving to remain in charge because it doesn't understand God's plan. But as you give each day's circumstances into God's hands, you can relax in his love and care, knowing that the God-centered approach to life is the most fulfilling.

THINKING IT THROUGH

1. Why do you think some people despair when confronted by the fact that life is out of their control ?

2. In what life circumstance have you lost control? Describe what happened and your reactions.

3. What evidence do you have that God can be trusted?

4. What do the following Bible passages indicate are the reasons we have for giving control to Christ?

   - Psalm 32:8
   - Psalm 40:5
   - Psalm 145:19
   - Proverbs 3:5-6
   - Daniel 4:34-35, 37
   - Matthew 6:33
   - Galatians 5:22-23
   - 1 Peter 5:7

5. What tends to keep you from yielding total control of your life to Christ?

6. Day by day, what can you do to give control to Christ?

2

Focus on the Kingdom

For in that kingdom there will be no preeminence and a man must have reached the stage of not caring two straws about his own status before he can enter it.   C. S. LEWIS

IRAQ'S invasion of Kuwait unleashed a sequence of events that few could have predicted. Saddam Hussein's ambitious plans to occupy oil-rich Kuwait would be the first line drawn in the sand, forcing ancient kingdoms to redefine their allegiances.

The Hashemite kingdom of Jordan was trapped in a no-win situation, trying to maintain a delicate balance of nonbelligerence toward their largest economic benefactor, Iraq, and at the same time not inflame the ire of the coalition forces.

As war ascended like a Sahara sunrise, the world watched intently for the latest fragment of news coming from the top of the Intercontinental Hotel in downtown Amman.

Few people watching those reports knew that a small Christian community in Amman was quietly but effectively having a profound impact in the shadow of these colossal events. It helped feed and give shelter to hundreds of thousands of refugees fleeing from Iraq during the time preceding Desert Storm. The Christians helped dispense medicine and offered a word of comfort and kindness in the name of Christ.

Among those who labored unselfishly was the Issam Ghattas family. They tirelessly prepared and distributed food and Christian literature. The oldest son, Paul, used his impeccable English to interpret for Dan Rather and other CBS correspondents in Amman during the war. His two sisters, Ronya and Rula, worked from dawn to dusk in the food lines. While they worked, the family felt the tension and stress of uncertainty about their future.

In their bedroom, during the late hours of night, the two sisters would talk. Death was the inescapable subject of their conversation:

"Before I die, I'd like to do more traveling. What about you?" Ronya asked.

"I'd like to get married and raise a family before dying," Rula answered.

For weeks, almost everyone in the Middle East was consumed with thoughts about death. Scud missiles, chemical warfare, and cluster bombs were the weapons discussed daily in the press and on television. Jordan was caught in the middle. Each missile aimed at Israel had to fly over Jordan, and if one should happen to fall a hundred miles short of its target. . . . It wasn't a pleasant thought.

To escape their thoughts about death, the two sisters began to dream of vacations without war. From their small, unpretentious home in the heart of the Hashemite kingdom, they giggled about going to the Magic Kingdom at Walt Disney World.

Two Different Kingdoms

Several months later the dream of these sisters came true. They flew to Orlando and not only visited Walt Disney World but also were given a VIP tour of the Disney underground by Bob Wacker, vice president of Human Resources. In a matter of days, these two sisters were touched by two different kingdoms. One kingdom was defined by geographical boundaries, a common language and religion, a cultural ethos, and historical linkage. The other kingdom created its definition through corporate goals, the vision of the founder and high-level officers, common values, and the language and mentality of stage performers. Each has a membership of varying degrees of loyalty. One group pledges allegiance to the national imperatives, the other to uphold the image of the corporate ideal.

Me? In a Kingdom?

We don't often think of ourselves as part of a kingdom. To belong to a kingdom sounds like something more akin to the animated Disney film *Aladdin* and the mythical Arabian kingdom of Agrabah. We Americans are rugged individuals. We each have a right to make our own decisions. But one of the keys to a dedicated Christian life is having a kingdom perspective.

Many types of kingdoms compete for our allegiance, and we may be members of several different kingdoms. Let's examine three: cultural, religious, and national. Each has a set of rules that governs the behavior of its subjects.

19

A Cultural Kingdom

"Sir, you can't wear those shorts," the man behind the counter of the Isleworth Country Club told me. "You'll have to put these on." His attitude wasn't highbrow but matter-of-fact. Rules were rules. I was wearing midthigh-length shorts, and Isleworth required knee-length shorts.

Even a golf course has a cultural kingdom! If you violate the cultural expectations of any particular group, you risk being ostracized. Just try playing golf at a country club wearing cutoff jeans and a Metallica T-shirt! To prevent their customers undue embarrassment and a wasted trip, most golf clubs have extra pairs of shorts and extra shirts available under the counter.

A country like ours includes a variety of cultures and subcultures. Some of these cultures are distinguished through economics, for example, and the various economic strata have their own rules for acceptance. Those of each culture can be seen attending their own social functions, wearing clothes and driving cars peculiar to that subculture. They follow defined rules of behavior for their subculture or kingdom.

A Religious Kingdom

If you ask people about their faith, some may tell you they belong to a certain church, such as First Baptist, or to a denomination, such as Presbyterian. That church or denomination is their kingdom. It's easy to spot people who belong to the same group. They speak a common language and abide by similar behavioral codes. They use in-house jargon, tell the same jokes (all of which have been tested for acceptability), and sometimes even wear the same kind of clothes. But often what looks similar in public can be widely different in the private realm.

When a major denomination was planning its national convention, one of the convention planners asked the hotel manager, "Are you going to close the bar since this group doesn't drink?"

"Oh no," the manager said, "room service will be great!"

The hotel manager knew from experience that this particular group had a public set of behavioral standards and a completely different private set. He was up-to-date on the cultural dynamics.

A National Kingdom

Each of us belongs to a geographical kingdom. Under normal conditions, we take for granted our national loyalty. But every four years, this loyalty is fiercely displayed in the Olympic games. Through the elaborate opening and closing ceremonies, each country, whether large or small, displays its uniforms, local costumes, and flag. Watching these talented youth proudly competing for the glory of the sport and country can be an invigorating experience. These young people are expected to be patriotic.

Unfortunately, sometimes the darker side of nationalism can be seen in marks subjectively given in events such as figure skating. If you closely monitor the judges, often one judge will consistently give lower marks to skaters from competing countries than he will give to skaters from his or her own country. For these judges, a sense of nationalism overrides a sense of fairness.

On a rare day, nationalism melts away into the shadows when a human drama compels a more grand response. During the 1994 Winter Olympics in Lillehammer, Norway, Dan Jansen from the United States slipped and lost his bid for a medal in the five-hundred-meter speed skating event. Going into the event, Jansen was the highest-ranked speed skater in the world. Lillehammer was his third Olympics and his final chance to win a medal.

Jansen's last attempt would be the thousand-meter race. With the crack of the starter's pistol, he lunged forward into his powerful, graceful form and was cheered by his fellow Americans as well as hundreds of screaming Norwegians. No one questioned the crowd's allegiance. They were simply cheering for another human being who was giving his energy to overcome the tragedies and misfortunes of his past. All who cheered set aside their national kingdom loyalties.

Where Is Your Loyalty?

When it comes to following Christ and the Word of God, anyone who is committed to God faces a dilemma, a loyalty test. Just how far should we carry our commitment?

It's one thing to believe in Jesus Christ out of our own need to find meaning and purpose. Jesus fills an aching hole in our soul and allows us to be released from the guilt baggage that has crippled us for years.

Yet, when we move beyond the initial step of belief, what happens when our loyalties are in direct conflict? Before we can understand these divided loyalties, we need to examine what Jesus said about the kingdom of God.

Jesus Christ talked about a kingdom-oriented life using both attractive and harsh statements. "Seek first his kingdom and his righteousness, and all these things will be given to you as well" (Matthew 6:33) sounds good—as if Jesus has a social-security plan for all of his followers. However, the mood changes when he says, "Anyone who loves his father or mother more than me is not worthy of me; anyone who loves his son or daughter more than me is not worthy of me" (Matthew 10:37). By stating what he did, Jesus gave us one of the distinctions of a committed Christian: Our loyalty to God must be exclusive. Jesus is not just someone to add to a "Top Ten" list of your favorite people or projects. Christianity isn't tried on like a new suit or test-driven like a new car. Christianity has a nonnegotiable sticker price.

To be committed Christians, we must ask hard questions about our ultimate loyalties to see if they parallel the priorities of the kingdom of God.

Four Kingdom Stories from Jesus

To help his audience understand the kingdom of God, Jesus told four stories, comparing the kingdom to a buried seed, a mustard seed, yeast, and a treasure. His parables also apply to us in our current century.

The Kingdom Is like a Buried Seed

> This is what the kingdom of God is like. A man scatters seed on the ground. Night and day, whether he sleeps or gets up, the seed sprouts and grows, though he does not know how. All by itself the soil produces grain—first the stalk, then the head, then the full kernel in the head. As soon as the grain is ripe, he puts the sickle to it, because the harvest has come. *Mark 4:26-29*

After a seed is planted, it looks lost, insignificant, and forgotten. But as it is hidden beneath the ground, the biological clock keeps ticking. The code for growth is uninterrupted, regardless if nobody notices. Then one day, from a crack in the earth, a small, tender shoot reaches for the warmth of the sun.

The same is true with God's kingdom. Sometimes it looks impotent when compared to armies, corporations, or other social institutions that visibly alter the landscape of our world. People often snicker about or sneer at the foolish and futile actions of the body of Christ. But the kingdom seed isn't dead. Silently and mysteriously, the Spirit of God is nourishing spiritual seed buried deep in the hearts of people who have responded to his call. When we least expect it, in the middle of a hostile environment, we marvel at a life transformed by God's grace, and it is infectious.

From time to time, the world gets a small glimpse of the kingdom growth. They learn of a Mother Teresa, working for years in an impoverished, hidden, and forgotten section of

Calcutta. Although there are millions of others working for God's kingdom, most of them are not very visible to the world. But one day these people will produce wonderful grain, whether or not they are ever recognized by the media.

The Kingdom Is like a Mustard Seed

The kingdom of heaven is like a mustard seed, which a man took and planted in his field. Though it is the smallest of all your seeds, yet when it grows, it is the largest of garden plants and becomes a tree, so that the birds of the air come and perch in its branches. *Matthew 13:31-32*

We should never despise small beginnings. Twelve men who walked with Jesus Christ turned the world upside down.

History is replete with stories of faithful people who planted seeds of God's kingdom in another country. Sometimes these people labored for years without seeing visible results. But eventually the seed took root and flourished. The church in every culture and nation outside of Palestine is a living testimony that the seeds of the kingdom have grown into trees.

Coach Bill McCartney of the Colorado Buffaloes football team began with the seed-thought of discipling men. Four years later, through prayer, planning, and promotion, this dream became a reality. McCartney launched Promise Keepers, an organization that challenges men to live up to their godly responsibilities as husbands, fathers, and employees. Over fifty thousand men jammed into Folsom Stadium at the University of Colorado with the sole purpose of following Jesus Christ.

Now Promise Keepers is dreaming of an army of men to break down the walls of racism. This organization is the largest interdenominational effort in America to embrace the entire brotherhood of Christ.

The Promise Keepers movement is a picture of kingdom growth from a seed to a tree, compressed into a short time frame.

The Kingdom Is like Yeast

> The kingdom of heaven is like yeast that a woman took and mixed into a large amount of flour until it worked all through the dough. *Matthew 13:33*

As yeast is added to dough, a fermentation process takes place, permeating everything. The kingdom of God is similar. It is not locked away for one day of the week or in one segment of society. The impact it makes wherever it goes cannot be stopped.

The ongoing process is the same within the kingdom follower. When believers go to work, they take the kingdom with them. The kingdom of God follows believers everywhere: into government, hospitals, the military, the world of sports, marriage, etc. The only way to stop such action would be to pass a law that prohibits believers from leaving home!

The Kingdom Is like a Treasure

> The kingdom of heaven is like treasure hidden in a field. When a man found it, he hid it again, and then in his joy went and sold all he had and bought that field. Again, the kingdom of heaven is like a merchant looking for fine pearls. When he found one of great value, he went away and sold everything he had and bought it. *Matthew 13:44-46*

Businesspeople love a good investment. If the investment gives a guaranteed rate of return, the businessperson knows it's a safe deal. If that same investment far exceeds the expected return, then it's a great deal.

Investment in the kingdom of God is not only safe and great, it is the best investment in the universe.

Why would people turn down an investment like this? Maybe they've never heard about it. Possibly it's socially unacceptable. Maybe it sounds too good to be true. Perhaps it just doesn't register. But Jesus offers—free of charge— eternal life and purpose and meaning in this life. It is all ours for the asking, 100 percent guaranteed. What a gold mine!

What Is Your Kingdom Strategy?

If we are committed to living a God-honoring life, we must decide on a kingdom strategy as we enter each sector of society. Not every location is a platform for a sermon. So how will we look for opportunities to share our faith and to bring up God's good news of hope with fellow employees and family members?

Our response depends on which of the following three strategies we choose as we interact with the world:

Strategy #1: Rejection

Some people believe that a Christian should attempt to avoid any contact with the outside world. People who adopt this strategy reject the culture of non-Christians because of the contamination it brings on them and their families. People with a rejection mind-set will never be contaminated by society; but they won't make a positive contribution to it either. It's difficult for someone to be "the salt of the earth" when the salt never leaves the saltshaker.

Strategy #2: Reform

Reformers want to change things. They have the perception that their agenda is truth, and they plan to bring the rest of the world up to speed. These reformers valiantly march into any institution with the intention to proclaim the message of Christ through their words and deeds. Every social contact is an opportunity to witness.

The enthusiastic actions of reformers have earned a response from society at large. The more zealous advocates of this viewpoint have scared many employers and the government into alarmist reactions. As a result, some want to prohibit public sharing of one's personal religious faith in order to protect people from "religious harassment." The social agenda espoused by many of the televangelists has startled many secularists who see themselves as potential captives in a serious declaration of war.

Though this view seems to line up with the evangelistic admonitions of Scripture, the advocates of this strategy see winning converts as the first step to controlling the agendas of all human institutions. But when converts or social structures don't fall or capitulate to the reformers' view, the reformers are set up for disappointment and possibly even disillusionment. Sadly, the adherents of this strategy can be tempted to reject the culture or see their faith as impotent if they don't transform social structures.

But we have a third option.

Strategy #3: Tension

Tension can be the healthy tautness between two competing ideologies. As long as there is tension, the two poles remain engaged in dialogue. Believers in Christ can create healthy tension when they offer their view of truth and life from a biblical perspective. They know that people can feel uncomfortable being challenged to think in ways that differ from the prevailing preferences of their world.

These believers want to salt the existing structures lightly and create an appealing flavor. They know that to dump the whole saltshaker in one place neither preserves nor flavors. It kills interest.

On February 28, 1994, the *Orlando Sentinel* printed a two-page article in the Style section entitled, "Religion in the

Workplace." The byline for the article said, "Going to work doesn't mean leaving faith at home. Employees are finding ways to balance their beliefs and jobs."

This article didn't bash Christians as being insulting reformers. It touted the validity of a person with strong religious beliefs. Those beliefs were valid and helpful when shared with a fellow worker deeply troubled by the normal crises of life. But the writer also pointed out potential pitfalls in sharing those beliefs:

> Religious people find different ways to deal with a very personal issue in the workplace. For instance, should they tell a coworker fraught with family problems they will keep them in their prayers? Do they say something and risk being considered judgmental when coworkers swear? . . . Sometimes a mention of religious underpinnings is greeted with surprise by those who are less spiritual or at least not as open about their spirituality. Tom Kohler, executive director of the Downtown Development Board in Orlando, sometimes shocks people when he tells them that becoming a Christian has changed his perspective on what's important. Sometimes, they're just taken aback and they say, "Oh," and they don't say, "Is that right? I'd like maybe to talk more about that."

Tom Kohler didn't declare war on the values of the *Orlando Sentinel,* and he did not try to turn it into a Christian publication. But thousands of readers got an appealing glimpse into the reality of the Christian life. As a kingdom-oriented Christian, Kohler showed that he knew how to handle the tension strategy.

What Does Being in the Kingdom Mean?
When we make a decision to accept Christ, we immediately

become a part of his family and his kingdom. As we learn more about godliness, we begin to adopt godly characteristics, the distinctions of the committed Christian. We change in many ways, becoming, in essence, new creatures. Being in God's kingdom means we have a new authority, new priorities, new relationships, a new lifestyle, new significance (a deeper purpose and meaning in life), and a new prize to pursue.

A New Authority

God's kingdom followers march to a different drummer. They may be loyal subjects of a country or other types of earthly kingdoms, but their first priority is the kingdom flag. Because of their commitment to God's kingdom, they have a heightened sense of responsibility to their local, state, and national leaders. They take seriously passages such as 1 Peter 2:13-14: "Submit yourselves for the Lord's sake to every authority instituted among men: whether to the king, as the supreme authority, or to governors, who are sent by him to punish those who do wrong and to commend those who do right."

People of the kingdom have a spiritual affinity with believers from every country of the world. They can no longer categorically hate all the citizens who come from a country that is considered a national enemy, even those that have declared war. A church exists in that country, a church Christ loves, made up of spiritual brothers and sisters.

During the Persian Gulf War, a small but devout group of believers in Jordan transported Bibles and other Christian literature to Iraq whenever they could. In the opening hours of the war, as I watched the Baghdad skyline light up with antiaircraft fire and the explosion of cruise missiles, I was emotionally schizophrenic. As a loyal American, I wanted to cheer our military on to victory without any loss of life. But then I thought, *What about those Christ followers who are now victims in this war?* I was torn between love for my country and love for the church in the Middle East. This is a hazard of being a kingdom follower. The tension will always exist for one whose heart embraces those under the authority of the King of kings.

The central tenet of democracy is "we the people" instead of "long live the king." The authority of our government is the authority of the majority. But in God's kingdom, the values are different. Most likely, it's more difficult for those of us who live in democratic countries to lay aside our "voting rights" in favor of unquestioned obedience to our Sovereign. But God didn't ask if we'd prefer a kingdom with less unilateral authority. He calls us to follow him on his terms or not at all.

Some Christians resist this new authority in their lives. They prefer to pick up mental scissors and snip out the parts of Scripture they don't like. They try to vote on guiding principles for their lives (similar to going to the polls every four years to elect a new governor). But snipping Scripture and voting on principles is a sure sign that a person really doesn't know what the kingdom of God is all about.

New Priorities

When I was working for Youth for Christ, I received this phone call: "Larry, we've got to get rid of Randy.[1] He's not working out." The accusations continued, and it was all I could do to continue listening. For many years, I had worked alongside Randy. I knew him to be a talented worker, deeply committed to Christ. I didn't deny there was a personnel problem, but the question was, How should I handle the situation as a committed Christian? The rules of the world would say to fire the man and be done with it. But kingdom-oriented believers handle these kinds of situations differently. At the risk of being misunderstood, I worked to solve the dilemma in a way that salvaged Randy's reputation and livelihood. Randy moved to another division within the ministry and proved to be a valuable asset. I was very grateful I had approached the situation with a kingdom mind-set rather than a standard formula for dealing with personnel problems.

Today the airwaves are full of talk about political correctness. In light of this new ethic, social mores are being redefined, and being politically correct has become the guiding priority for millions in this country. Society says that the past is unimportant. Importance is found in the majority opinion (or those who have political clout and think they are the majority). For years, Chuck Colson has been sounding the alarm regarding this train of thought: "But today truth is retreating. Today we are witnessing the abolition of truth. Since the 1960s in America, the reigning orthodoxy has been relativism—the belief that there is no absolute truth. This is absolutely rampant on our campuses in America today. One of the leading proponents of relativism—or deconstructionism, which is what it is called on our campuses—claims there is no objective meaning to what is written; what happened in the past has no significance; it only matters what we think about it today."[2]

One of the greatest dangers stemming from those who embrace the priorities of political correctness is that those who have the largest crowd behind their preferences, whether it is relativism or political correctness, will force their preferences on those who have the least power.

But kingdom followers get their priorities from the Bible—more specifically, the words of Christ in his Sermon on the Mount (Matthew 5:3-12). What priorities are these?

1. Kingdom people have a humble attitude. They're not just looking out for Number One.
2. Kingdom people acknowledge their need to be gentle, instead of trying to win through intimidation.

3. Kingdom people desire to please God. They want to hear "Well done, good and faithful servant."

4. Kingdom people desire to show mercy rather than demand an eye for an eye or a tooth for a tooth.

5. When kingdom people ultimately defeat egotism, they don't brag that they did it their way.

6. Kingdom people are not always trying to defend themselves. They can't be heard threatening others with "make my day."

7. Wholly, and without apology, kingdom people identify with Christ. They don't try to recreate him in the likeness of their own preferences.

New Relationships

As kingdom-oriented Christians, we pursue new relationships—even at the risk of our own social status.

Let's consider the story of the Prodigal Son, which is also a story about a "foolish in the world's eyes" father (Luke 15:11-32). A greedy, ungrateful son wishes his father were dead so he could receive his inheritance. This son insults his father, his family, and his home village by asking for his "share of the estate." A reasonable father in first century A.D. standards would have closed the door behind his son with a vow never to see him again.

But in the kingdom of God, the concerns of the culture or family take a backseat to the admonition of Jesus—love our enemies. In this story, the wandering son is the enemy. Yet what did the father do? He treated him as royalty, as an honored guest, and he threw a party reserved for only special occasions. The father lived according to the relationships of the kingdom, not the world.

There could have been negative consequences to this father's actions. The village patriarchs could have seen this as a dangerous precedent. What if other sons began asking to leave the village, with their wallets stuffed with their inheritance? Then the foolish father would become a threat to the entire village.

Our heavenly Father also throws a party for those who repent. Donald Kraybill, author of *The Upside-Down Kingdom*, describes God this way: "God is like a Jewish father who rewards his pork-eating son with steak. Instead of spanking the son who brings disgrace, he elevates him to the high post of 'most honored guest.' God is like a parent who asks no questions, even when treated as though dead. This is limitless, unconditional love with no strings attached."[3]

The priorities of the kingdom lead to a bold pursuing of relationships. As committed Christians, we take the time to build relationships and risk personal social status for the sake of these relationships. They become more central than accomplishments such as building edifices or organizations. Instead of the size of our budgets or staffs, Christianity is about expressing love—across cultures, across racial distinctions, and across economic barriers.

The Lupton family lives in the inner city of Atlanta and works with FCS Urban Ministries. In this cross-cultural setting, the Luptons have exposed their children to different types of relationships and given them a kingdom orientation.

When the Atlanta Braves won the World Series in 1991, Jonathan, one of the Lupton sons, and two of his friends went downtown to celebrate. After enjoying the parade of players in the streets, they headed back to their car.

Suddenly they were surrounded by African Americans. An elbow jammed into Jonathan's head and knocked him to the ground. The crowd turned and kicked the young man with a viciousness that he didn't understand. He curled into a fetal position until a stranger lifted him upright and moved him out of the crowd.

"Do you want to go to the hospital?" friends Susan and Ashok asked repeatedly.

"No," Jonathan gasped. "It's not that bad."

Yet inside Jonathan was asking, *How will I feel when I get back home and my black friends and neighbors greet me? Will I be afraid of them? Will this turn me into a racist and destroy my relationships with the community?*

The next day on his high school bus, the air tingled with excitement. He was among friends and acquaintances, but he was the only white person in the crowd. Several seats in front, a couple of friends were giggling about some white guy who had been beaten the night before.

"That was me," Jonathan said. At first, the students around him roared out loud; they thought it was a joke. But when Jonathan didn't join the laughter, the mood turned serious. Suddenly a bruised white boy wasn't just a story; he was a friend who had come close to being a victim of mob violence.

Many people would consider the Luptons foolish for exposing their family to the dangers of the inner city. But in response to God's call, they continue to build a network of relationships as faithful representatives of the kingdom. Those relationships are expanding, and now a large section of downtown Atlanta has seen a glimpse of what God had in mind when the kingdom is taken seriously.

New Lifestyles

In corporate kingdoms, following the company policy is rewarded with salary increases and responsibility promotions. In the military kingdom, reward is a medal or a promotion in rank. In the kingdom of God, committed Christians are rewarded with a new sense of satisfaction for their lives. Each day we can rejoice that our lives count for eternal significance. We gain a new lifestyle—no longer controlled by money or sex, but characterized by discipline.

Not controlled by money. Jim Bakker of the PTL Club received top media coverage when he became snared in the symbols and rewards of the ministry. Materialism and money became his measure for success. How many television stations could he reach? How many millions could he raise? As his audience increased in size, he had the power to call famous people and to travel wherever he wanted. But money, success, and power led to his downfall.

You can sense Jesus' sadness when he talked with a rich young man in Mark 10:17-23. Outwardly the man was a model of faithfulness, yet his true allegiance was his pursuit and control of wealth. Jesus didn't question how the young man had obtained his money; that wasn't the point. He knew that riches had become the dominating motivator in this young man's life. God allows no room for competition in his kingdom.

The wealthy are not the only people to have problems with money. Often people without money think of nothing else and fall into the same trap. If we have a kingdom orientation, we will have a new lifestyle with goals that are not shaped by a desire for riches.

Not controlled by sex. The lifestyle of kingdom followers is free from entanglements in sexual sins. Christians aren't prudish, maladjusted Bible thumpers with Victorian ideals. They realize the pressures and temptations that face all warm-blooded humans. They know the attraction of good-looking, intelligent, humorous, and well-proportioned members of the opposite sex.

Armed with such knowledge, they deliberately avoid any circumstance that would put them in a compromising position. They don't subscribe to movie channels or magazines that exploit sexual appetites. They don't use people to satisfy their basic urges—or for any reason.

Characterized by discipline. A third characteristic of a kingdom follower's lifestyle is that of personal discipline. The apostle Paul said, "Do you not know that the wicked will not inherit the kingdom of God? Do not be deceived: Neither the sexually immoral nor idolaters nor adulterers nor male prostitutes nor homosexual offenders nor thieves nor the greedy nor drunkards nor slanderers nor swindlers will inherit the kingdom of God. And that is what some of you were" (1Corinthians 6:9-11).

The world around us is full of shady characters. Everyone has a special list of attributes that would keep them off the guest list to a Puritan party. Paul is not saying that anyone who ever sinned should be blacklisted from the kingdom. Committed Christians, according to Paul, have a changed set of priorities and activities. The addictions and temptations of the past no longer control them. God's kingdom is full of nonparticipating idolaters, adulterers, homosexuals, thieves, money grubbers, drunkards, and gossipers who are now controlled and disciplined because of their love and commitment to Christ.

New Significance

The significance of those in the kingdom comes from their irrevocable call to be a child of God (Romans 11:29). God uses the terminology of royalty to describe our relationship to him: "But you are a chosen people, a royal priesthood, a holy nation, a people belonging to God, that you may declare the praises of him who called you out of darkness into his wonderful light" (1 Peter 2:9).

No one in the kingdom is excluded from these privileges. And every believer is given spiritual gifts for the body. But many feel their skills are dwarfed by the visible spiritual giants that receive public acclaim. How can an average person make a meaningful contribution? As Steve Arterburn and Jack Felton write in *Toxic Faith,*

They become lazy in their service and are not motivated to find a way to further the kingdom of God. They neglect the gifts God has given them because they are not as great as others. They view themselves as inferior believers. In my life as well as in Scripture, I have seen nothing but the opposite to be true. God often uses those who have major flaws or who have been through a great deal of pain to accomplish many vital tasks for His kingdom. Look at Moses the stutterer, Paul with his thorn in the flesh, and David the adulterer. It seems that God uses the "spiritual giants" despite their flaws.[4]

When we become kingdom followers, we have new purpose and meaning in life—from Christ alone.

Because my family lived in Houston for fifteen years, we became attached to the Houston Oilers football team. Our loyalty became stronger during the reign of Coach Bum Phillips and running back Earl Campbell, even after a series of disappointing play-off games.

No Oilers fan can ever forget the 1992 game with the Buffalo Bills. Houston was leading at halftime by the lopsided score of 32-3. All they had to do was not give up twenty-nine points in two quarters of football, and they were on their way to the divisional play-offs. At the beginning of the second half, Buffalo substituted Frank Reich for Jim Kelly; Reich would lead his team to the greatest comeback in NFL history.

The rest of the world didn't know about the internal struggles Frank Reich had faced the week before the game. As a Christian he knew his identity and significance were in Christ, but the last time Buffalo had played Houston, Frank had not performed well. He had many self-doubts, like anyone who felt he had let down his teammates. Reich was determined to live up to his potential.

On Wednesday before the wild-card game, Frank received a

phone call from his sister: "Frank, you've got to listen to this new CD, especially the song 'In Christ Alone.'"

After Frank heard the song, he broke down and sobbed. The words reflected his deep yearning to allow Christ to receive the glory for his successes. He wanted to be victorious on the kingdom team, regardless of his week-to-week performance on the football field. On game day, Frank went out to his car, turned on the window defroster, and waited for his windshield to clear. He listened to the song again, this time writing down the words.

When the halftime festivities were over, Frank took his position as the quarterback. He didn't focus on the overwhelming odds of a comeback victory. He didn't even primarily focus on scoring touchdowns. He kept his eye on one target at a time, throwing one completed pass after another. The momentum of the game shifted. When time ran out at the end of regulation play, the score was tied. A Buffalo field goal completed the legacy of the afternoon.

The Buffalo locker room was a riot of ecstasy. Players were screaming, hugging, and knocking each other to the floor in unbridled joy. One of Frank's friends came to him and said the press was waiting for a postgame interview. Frank flashed back to the words of the song he had written down before the game. He began the interview by reading those words:

> *In Christ alone will I glory,*
> *Though I could pride myself in battles won.*
> *For I've been blessed beyond measure,*
> *And by His strength alone I overcome.*
> *Oh, I could stop and count successes*
> *Like diamonds in my hand,*
> *But those trophies could not be equal*
> *To the grace by which I stand.*

Chorus:
In Christ alone I place my trust
And find my glory in the power of the cross.
In every victory let it be said of me,
My source of strength,
My source of hope,
Is Christ alone.

In Christ alone will I glory,
For only by His grace I am redeemed.
And only His tender mercy
Could reach beyond my weakness to my need.
Now, I seek no greater honor
Than just to know Him more
And to count my gains but losses
And to the glory of my Lord.[5]

Frank Reich is a kingdom man. His significance has nothing to do with victory or defeat on the field. Neither the agony nor the ecstasy of life's experiences can alter the realities of his relationship to the Captain of his soul.

New Prize

The Frank Reich story also illustrates how kingdom priorities don't fade once the stadium is empty and the cheering becomes a faint memory.

Many people set their hearts on prizes that either tarnish with time or don't bring fulfillment. For example, the political arena is very alluring, and power is a difficult narcotic to overcome. But the prizes of "office" fade.

Even the religious world has its own corporate and bureaucratic structure that, for some, outshines the original motive to love God and serve people. The past two thousand years provide a history lesson on the corruptibility of clergy and ecclesiastical organizations. When pastors lose sight of the kingdom, they can be seduced by exciting peripherals and create multilevels of bureaucratic nonsense for themselves and the laity. Then their personal kingdoms receive all of the attention while a hurting world stands outside and watches with disdain. In effect, corruption in the religious world serves to turn many people away from the God who is longing to reach them. We are called to reach out to this hurting world with compassion.

A Heart for the World

Once you have decided to become a kingdom Christian, you can do many things to develop a heart for the world.

You could go on a short-term missions trip. Hundreds of churches and parachurch organizations sponsor one- or two-week excursions to nearly every country on earth. You will meet people whose needs are unimaginably desperate. But you will often find that these same people will extend to you hospitality that would make Americans feel inadequate.

You can volunteer to work for a missions agency that has its home office in your area. You can collect food, medicine, clothes, or other items the agency needs to fulfill its mission. If you want to get even more involved, express your interest in serving on the mission agency's board of directors. When missionaries are invited to speak at your church, offer to let them stay at your house. Exposing your children to these special people will do wonders for their worldview.

Every church's missions committee needs volunteers. You can study about the work your congregation supports. You can begin to correspond with missionaries and ask them what you can do to help ease their burdens. I recently experienced this kind of personal caring. A church that contributes to The Gathering USA wrote and asked what else they could provide to help increase the organization's effectiveness. It was the first time I had ever received that kind of letter in my nearly twenty years of service. I nearly fainted!

The Bottom Line

Being a kingdom-oriented believer may not sound all that exciting, but it is one of the most rewarding of all the characteristics listed in this book. As you seek to know more about the kingdom of Christ in your neighborhood and around the world, you'll learn how various people from different cultures live out their faith on a day-to-day basis. You'll see new levels of spiritual commitment and be challenged by new visions of how the Christian message of hope can impact the world.

It's not a pain-free process. Unfortunately, you'll realize how self-absorbed many Christians are and how little some churches do to empower believers in other countries. Although these situations may not radically change, *you will change.* God will use your reshaped priorities to touch people in ways you didn't even know were possible!

THINKING IT THROUGH

1. Make a list of the "kingdoms" to which you belong:

   - physical
   - social
   - religious
   - cultural

2. What impresses you the most about the kingdom of God? Why?

3. Of the three strategies for relating to the world—rejection, reform, tension—which one do you adopt? Why? How does this affect the way you approach others for Christ?

4. What do the following passages teach you about kingdom living?

- Matthew 4:23
- Matthew 5:3, 10, 20
- Matthew 6:10
- Mark 4:11-12
- Mark 10:14, 23
- Luke 9:62
- Luke 17:20-21
- John 18:36
- Galatians 5:19-21

5. Which of your personal loyalties might be in competition with God's kingdom? How will you adjust those in the coming weeks to give God first priority in your life?

3

Put Others First in a "Me First" World

We all have a lurking desire to be exhibitions for God, to be put, as it were, in his showroom. Jesus does not want us to be specimens, he wants us to be so taken up with him that we never think about ourselves. OSWALD CHAMBERS

HAVE you ever made a lasting impression? One man made a lasting impression that changed his future.

President William McKinley was considering two different men for a coveted position as ambassador of the United States in another country. Both candidates were almost equal.

As President McKinley thought about the men, he remembered an incident when he served in the House of Representatives. On a crowded streetcar, McKinley located a seat in the back. A man boarded the streetcar and took the last vacant seat. Then a woman with a heavy basket of laundry got on the car and stood next to the man who had just sat down. To avoid seeing the woman and her basket, the man shifted his newspaper and refused to give up his seat. That man was one of the candidates McKinley was considering.

"I never told this man about his selfish action and what it cost him," President McKinley said. "But I didn't select him as an ambassador for the United States."

Self-Interest: Our Natural Tendency

When people are rude, they appear either thoughtless or ignorant. A popular television figure today is the self-centered husband Homer Simpson. The "Archie Bunker" of the nineties, Homer perches in his comfortable chair and tells his wife, Marge, "Beer me." That's the signal for Marge to turn to the refrigerator and obediently get a beer for Homer. We laugh at Homer's audacity to be so self-centered, yet in some ways he models the actions of the world around us. How do we keep from acting like a Christian version of Homer Simpson?

Considering others first certainly doesn't come naturally. Tune in to the Discovery Channel if you want to see how the beasts of nature handle it. The hidden cameras reveal a horrifying example of looking out for number one. If a wild animal didn't think of itself, it wouldn't live past sundown.

Humans should be able to escape the survival-of-the-fittest mode of operation. But humans can be remarkably brutal, creating hellish ways to annihilate each other. The Nazis of World War II didn't invent genocide. It has been around since the development of the tribal social order. The modern-day massacres of the Bosnian people and the intertribal bloodbath of Rwanda are other examples of unbridled self-absorption.

During the first few months of life, we begin to express our self-interest. Drop by a child-care center and watch seven- or eight-month-old infants crawling on the floor. They know what toy they want, and they go after it. If they think they have been bypassed when others are being fed, look out. You are about to get an earful.

As adults, we may feel we've grown beyond self-absorption. Here's a simple test to find out: When a group photo is passed around, who is the first person you look for?

Competition: Good or Bad?

Business, politics, and sports thrive on competition, and competitiveness provides one of the greatest tests of our attitude toward others. Competition works only when there are winners and losers.

The competitive edge can provide tremendous motivation for people to develop discipline, set goals, learn perseverance, use natural skills, and feel the pride of accomplishment. But competition can also be the training ground for hostile aggression. Some years ago, when I helped a Christian who was running for political office, I sat in on strategy sessions and listened to those with political savvy discuss the opponent as if he were the devil incarnate. Constantly, my candidate was fed information to discredit and annihilate the other person on the ticket. While I didn't support the opposition, I was in touch with what this process began to do to me. The opponent became the enemy. I discovered how hard it is to love your enemy and to wish him or her well. Although I was told that politics works with a "them vs. us" mentality and that if we were to influence the state with our values, we had to play hardball just as every other successful candidate did, I didn't agree. And I didn't last long in that arena.

Many professional athletes face similar situations in the sports world. Some coaches and owners complain that athletes can't measure up to their potential on the field of competition if they embrace the Sermon on the Mount. Perhaps this view arises out of preconceived, stereotypical images of spineless and nonaggressive Christians. This myth is shattered by scores of Christian professional athletes who have been recognized as true champions.

However, all Christians still need to make a decision about competition. In contact sports, the push to win has led to the cheap shot. Games are filled with intentional, flagrant fouls, clothesline tackles, bench-clearing brawls, suspensions, and fines. The Christian athlete has some soul-searching to do, as does the Christian politician and anyone else who deals with day-to-day competition. We have to decide whether we will adopt the biblical attitude about competition or the prevailing view of the culture.

The Biblical View: Others-Centered

The apostle Paul used the analogy of a race to illustrate his personal standards for discipline and growth. He engaged in competition with his own ideals about spiritual achievement. The winners would be everyone he influenced through his personal example: "Do you not know that in a race all the runners run, but only one gets the prize? Run in such a way as to get the prize. Everyone who competes in the games goes into strict training. They do it to get a crown that will not last; but we do it to get a crown that will last forever. Therefore I do not run like a man running aimlessly; I do not fight like a man beating the air. No, I beat my body and make it my slave so that after I have preached to others, I myself will not be disqualified for the prize" (1 Corinthians 9:24-27).

Paul is saying we can either be in or out of spiritual shape. Just as discipline is critical in preparing for a sporting event, the same is true in preparing to accomplish anything spiritually.

In the book of Hebrews, the writer uses the race analogy to describe the call of God for each believer: "Therefore, since we are surrounded by such a great cloud of witnesses, let us throw off everything that hinders and the sin that so easily entangles, and let us run with perseverance the race marked out for us" (Hebrews 12:1-2).

Athletes are careful to wear just the right equipment. On the day of their competition, the last thing they want to think about is whether they are adequately clothed or protected. Likewise, believers who are serious about spiritual accomplishments will say no to anything that limits their advantage and yes to anything that enhances it.

This puts Christian taboos in a new light. Christian athletes eliminate unhealthy foods, erotic stimulants, and addictive substances, not because they are killjoys, but because those taboos shave off their effectiveness. Besides, there's a stadium full of spectators they don't want to disappoint!

Competition in the Bible

At least three times in the Gospels we see the nasty side of the competitive ego, which is always furthered at the expense of someone else.

The widow vs. wealthy donors (Mark 12:41-44). When Jesus walked into the temple, he found a place where he could watch as people made donations into the temple treasury. Some people deposited large amounts. Then a widow came with two small copper coins. While this section of Scripture doesn't judge the wealthy donors for being hypocritical, Jesus says their contribution was only a tip from their abundance.

Acts of charity can become a type of competition among Christians who think giving is a means of looking good. Some people who give want others to be aware of their generosity. Perhaps that's why there are named sections of hospitals and dedication plaques on public buildings. Some people keep track of the giving of others so their gift will be respected; others give because the cause is worthy. They may receive deserved publicity, but they didn't seek it.

In the story of the copper coins, the real winner is the widow. Her small contribution wins the giving contest hands down, although proportionately it doesn't even compare with the others. She gives, completely unaware of competition.

Donation games are played in secular organizations and in churches as well. Some programs play toward ego-stroking, recognizing specific donors for giving, knowing the money would not come in without giving donors special attention. Like an ESPN wrap-up after the big game, Jesus gives a post-event commentary on this situation: "This poor widow has put more into the treasury than all the others."

The Pharisee vs. the tax collector (Luke 18:9-14). Jesus told a parable about two men who went to the temple to pray. The tax collector humbled himself and asked God for mercy, while the Pharisee proudly compared himself with the tax collector, saying, in essence, "I'm glad I'm not like that guy."

Some Christians take great delight in comparing themselves against a dark, evil background. Proud and puffed up, these people observe the rest of the world and decide they're not so bad. In fact, by comparison, they're good. It's a contest of performance and accomplishments: fasting, praying, giving, and doing vs. acts of shame and embarrassment.

The contest might be compared to a boxing match. The Pharisee enters the ring dressed in silver robes. As he pirouettes in his fine attire for the audience, the Pharisee thanks God for his good fortune. The tax collector, however, slides between the ropes and cowers in the corner. You can't see what he is saying, but you know he is whispering something. With one hand he thumps his breast, then asks the referee for mercy. The final bell sounds; the referee grabs the arm of each and lifts the tax collector's in victory. He announces to the stunned crowd, "For everyone who exalts himself will be humbled, and he who humbles himself will be exalted."

When competition elevates one person at the expense of the other, both are headed for a surprise ending.

James and John vs. the other ten disciples (Mark 10:35-45). Toward the end of Jesus' life, James and John asked for a special favor. They wanted to be seated at the right and left of Jesus in heaven. When the other disciples overheard this request, they became indignant.

Self-absorbed people want special treatment. If there is a line, they want to be first. If there is a platform, they want to be seated in the middle of it. If there is a first-class status, they want to be included. The rules for others don't apply to them. Their feelings of success come when others are beneath them, socially or economically.

James and John wanted those honored seats so they could feel like winners. After their request, Jesus gave the qualifications for the seats of honor—leave high-minded lording tactics behind, quit trying to act like a big shot, and start serving all the people you are competing against. "Whoever wants to be first must be slave of all."

Portrait of a "Me First" Person

Ernest Hemingway's parents came from a strong Christian lineage in Oak Park, Illinois. His paternal grandfather served the YMCA as general secretary and developed a lasting friendship with evangelist Dwight L. Moody. Ernest's uncle worked overseas as a missionary physician in China. Hemingway's father, Dr. C. E. Hemingway, practiced medicine. Along with his wife, Grace, Dr. Hemingway demanded strict obedience to the Christian faith. To give the Hemingway children a lasting impression of the consequences of sin, they carted them off to visit the state prison. There the children could see and feel the harshness of iron bars and barbed wire.

As an adolescent, Ernest read every word of the King James Bible to win a Bible-reading contest. At fourteen, he played the lead role in a Sunday school play at the Third Congregational Church of Oak Park. But near the end of his life he said, "I live in a vacuum that is as lonely as a radio tube when the batteries are dead and there is no current to plug into." Somewhere between early adulthood and the Sunday in 1961 when he blew his brains out in the Sawtooth Mountains of Idaho, he rejected the Christianity of his parents. Instead, Hemingway embraced an all-out pursuit of adventure, hunting, fishing, eating, and drinking with friends—anything that would bring pleasure. He measured life with what he experienced, what he absorbed. Eventually the glass from which he drank consumed him.

Dr. George Balentine said, "The smallest package in the world is the one who wraps himself up in himself." Ernest Hemingway was selfish. If he had exchanged his selfish pursuits for a heart large enough to embrace others, the vacuum tubes in his radio would never have gone cold.

Selfish Manners

As I sat in the audience of the National Youth for Christ Convention in San Francisco, Dr. Francis Schaeffer shared how he felt the Western world was quickly losing its Christian memory. The spiritual values taught by relatives had vanished, and now there was no connection to the Bible. One of the first indications of this lost trait was the vanishing of manners. To have manners, people don't have to be moral or spiritual. They just need to remember how moral and spiritual people behave, then imitate them. But when there's no memory, there's no need to act mannerly.

Although people may claim to be Christians, their manners may exhibit a preoccupation with self. Here are some of the characteristics of a self-absorbed, unmannerly person.

They are intolerant. Selfish people treat their own needs as a priority, and they don't care about the feelings of others.

They feel they should be free from those who are troubled, depressed, or worried. They don't tolerate anyone whose moods aren't in sync with their own. Sometimes these people object to another viewpoint, even if it is accurate, because the idea didn't originate with them. Who gets the credit for good ideas is extremely important to an intolerant person.

They can't listen. "Yeah, let me talk." While self-absorbed people may not verbally say these words, the idea comes across in their actions. They can't listen because they are waiting for their chance to speak. Another person's conversation is an opportunity for their own oration, so they often hurry the words out of your mouth.

They are perfectionists. Perfection isn't a bad word. It is okay to maintain perfection in some areas. However, others turn perfection into a sickness. They want to avoid the appearance of failure at all costs. They become demanding and overbearing. Their preoccupation with self doesn't allow them to be human. Often this type of person is searching for personal impurities so they can purge them and move to a higher spiritual plane. In reality, they are struggling with an inverted form of pride.

They don't share the load. "Laziness" is another word for this characteristic. Let's say a working husband comes home and flops down on the couch in front of a ball game on television, forgetting his stay-at-home wife has carried the majority of the housework and child care for the day. Or perhaps a worker refuses to do anything more than his or her job description while another coworker carries an unfair burden.

They don't think before speaking or leaping. Selfish people don't consider the ramifications of words. In order to feel better, they are compelled—even encouraged by psychologists—to "spill their guts" in open confrontation with parents, spouse, friends, or the boss. If they suppress these emotions, they are termed *psychologically disabled*. But such confrontations may disable many people in the process.

Not every confrontation is self-absorbed, however. Those who think of others first measure their words carefully, are aware of the importance of timing, and approach the situation in a loving and nonjudgmental way. They don't just unload on some poor person and then depart feeling better, while the victim has to deal with the verbal garbage.

One Sunday evening, as my wife and I drove through an adjoining subdivision, we came behind two fourteen-year-old boys who were riding their bikes in the center of the road. They refused to pull over to the side and let us pass. So we lumbered along at a snail's pace until we could finally pass on the extreme left. As we squeezed by, I rolled down my window to ask, "Why couldn't you let us by?" They answered with obscene hand gestures and shouts of foul language that could be heard throughout the entire neighborhood. My wife and I felt we had just had garbage dumped on us, and our pleasant drive was nearly ruined.

When Leaders Are Self-Centered

For a variety of reasons, leaders rise to the top of their field. Many have the skills needed to promote, raise money, manage, or attract followers that allow a Christian organization to prosper. Because of their skills, they are often treated as special; unfortunately, some grow to believe it. Although these leaders teach servanthood from the pulpit and even feign interest in others, inside they feel being nice is a waste of time.

Fortunately, it's difficult for self-centered leaders to fool people forever. But sadly, followers can be hurt when they realize their leader isn't sincere. They become angry, feel manipulated, and silently withdraw from further involvement in Christian activity.

If a leader is self-centered, the following five problems communicate loudly to everyone around that leader:

The Problem of Authoritarian Leaders

Strong leaders are needed to meet the challenges that face organizations every day. As one person said, "When people are floundering and there is no cohesive and clearly articulated vision, the last thing we need is group grope." Leadership gets things accomplished. But there is a difference between *authoritarian* and *decisive* leadership.

Authoritarian leaders believe that no one knows more than they do about where the organization should go. They feel they have been granted the license to set the exclusive course for action. Often they have ego-driven dreams and don't want anyone else to appear with an equally credible or, God forbid, superior idea. If these leaders are challenged, they act as if their credibility has been questioned. To them, acknowledging someone else's idea is a sign of weakness. In fact, if someone comes up with creative alternatives to the current course, he or she is directly challenged or manipulated into another position where his or her voice isn't heard. The people who side with the alternative viewpoint often keep quiet because they don't want a fight. These people also are concerned that if the authoritarian leader doesn't get his or her way, the leader will quit.

The Problem of Controlling Leaders

Delegating isn't in the vocabulary of controlling leaders— even when they find their workload overwhelming. They need to have the final say in every situation, and that need looms larger than their need for effectiveness. They think: *I'm key to keeping the ship afloat with my decision-making skills. I'm doing this for my people.* But inside they are only feeding their ego.

Whether we work in Christian education in a respected evangelical university or in a parachurch organization or local church, we can be blindsided by a self-absorbed egotist. Eventually, however, they will spring a leak. Like Saul in the book of 1 Samuel, these leaders are internally tortured by their duplicity. One day they utter ecstatic verbiage with the prophets of their day; the next they spew venom and murderous intent out of jealous rage.

In today's world, controlling leaders are crafty and creative. They know they can't appear to need power, and they can't exercise that power blatantly. Instead, they gain control through innuendo, through words that have double meaning. Or they invite followers into the inner circle of confidences to decipher their loyalty quotient, to find out what their followers really think about them. They create self-doubts in their followers and plant lies, like destructive mines, along the way to destroy some and corral others. Eventually, self-destruction is their payoff for appearing to be spiritually directed, when in reality they are self-consumed.

The Problem of Closed Communication

If Christian leaders reach the top and then lose touch with their people, it's because they don't really care about their followers. In their view, only communication that flows from the top down is legitimate because "it's the only way to get the job done."

Closed communication is especially evident when multiple layers of committees or advocacy groups lobby for the leader's interests. This type of leader pretends to listen. To make it look as if everyone is participating, the leader may even form special fact-finding groups. But somehow the recommendations from those groups tend to evaporate into thin air. Although committee members may feel their ideas were rejected in favor of better ideas, they don't realize they participated in an exercise of futility. The leader was manipulating them to achieve his or her own goals.

Why does this happen? The bottom line is that these leaders

develop selective hearing and respond only to those items that are important to their agenda. Unfortunately, these leaders' feelings of spiritual superiority are reinforced daily by the accolades from the general populace of followers. While such leaders may preach servanthood, they reduce their followers to insignificance by not listening. What a dehumanizing and ugly by-product of self-centeredness!

The Problem of Labeling People

"Those folks over there are the malcontents," this type of leader says. Lumping people into categories makes it easier to disregard them. It places distance between the person and the issue. It degrades the people labeled, making them inhuman and their opinions invalid. Through their own selfishness and lack of respect, "labeling leaders" avoid any legitimate input from groups because what they really want is control. Sometimes these leaders even withhold their contribution and ideas until the group follows their way. That's spiritual blackmail—and it's very much what the world does.

The secular media tends to lump all religious people into the "religious right" or the "fundamentalist fanatic fringe." Everyone is tarred with the same brush. The process doesn't single out an individual but makes it easier to hate the whole group.

Military complexes in every country use this same tactic. Soldiers find it hard to kill someone who is a person and has a family waiting at home. So the commanders label the enemy as "krauts," "frogs," "gooks," or "commies." Once labeled, these people fall into the same category as insects—with a need to be exterminated. The Nazis used the same labeling to portray the Jews. According to the hate propaganda, the Jews were nothing more than rodents.

Labeling tends to polarize the camp and energize the opposition. Anyone on the periphery of the conflict hears that the

"X group" is misled; they don't have the facts. Without know-ing what games are being played, many innocent people get agitated against the "X group" because of the way truth was defined to them. When leaders do not think of others first, they selectively control the flow of information, then cast aspersions on the opposition through denigrating labels.

The Problem of Programs over People

Many years ago, I was part of a team that was building an auditorium. As a group of men lacquered wall panels in as-sembly-line fashion, suddenly a large group of them fell like dominoes on a worker's arm. The director of the ministry and I sped to the hospital with the injured young man in the backseat of the car. During that trip, the director said to the boy, "Now you know this was your fault. We don't want to have any injury claims on our insurance policy." At that mo-ment and in that situation, programs were more important to that director than the welfare of an employee.

Some people consider the apostle Paul a driven, type A personality. They say he would walk over mountains or people (like John Mark) to achieve his mission. But these people confuse Paul's passion with drivenness. While Paul was a focused and determined achiever, he was also ex-tremely loyal to his coworkers. During a mission trip to Troas, Paul found a warm reception and an open door to preach the gospel (2 Corinthians 2:12-13). Paul lived for this sort of opportunity, but something was wrong. He couldn't find Titus, so he left.

That's no means to build a ministry—leaving just when things start going well. But that action demonstrated the importance of Titus to Paul. Paul's larger strategy was to build himself into people like Titus, Archippus, Timothy, and Luke. Other than his relationship with Christ, the most important thing in Paul's life was ministering with and to his closest friends. The open door would have to wait until he found Titus.

Modern leaders can learn from Paul's example. Often they believe the program is king. They seem to have little concern about the people who are chewed up to add one more brick in their program. They've forgotten the attraction of the early church—that they cared for one another. Paul said love is the greatest attribute of mankind and that it surpasses faith— faith that can build worldwide movements with multimillion-dollar budgets. While such programs are impressive, Paul knew you don't impress people into the kingdom. You attract them with a magnet like love.

What Does It Mean to Put Others First?

Where can we turn for a modern-day example of someone focused on others? While it is fiction, the traits of a changed life are found in Henry Turner, played by Harrison Ford in the movie *Regarding Henry.* A self-absorbed New York lawyer, Henry successfully defended a hospital against a negligence suit from an elderly couple.

In the opening scenes, Henry has little time for his wife, Sarah, or his eleven-year-old daughter, Rachel—unless Rachel spills juice on the piano. But his family isn't the only one he neglects; he doesn't even acknowledge the doorman's greet-ings at his high-rise apartment.

One evening Henry enters a corner shop to buy a pack of cigarettes and surprises a gunman holding up the store. Henry can't talk his way out of this one. When the gunman shoots him in the head, the lack of oxygen from the bleeding causes brain damage. When Henry comes out of the surgery, he can't speak or move, and his memory is greatly affected.

Through the efforts of a tenacious therapist, Henry slowly regains the use of his limbs and learns to walk again. But his memory is gone, and he doesn't know his family. Coaxed into returning home, Henry has a tough mental transition. Everything about his life has changed. When Henry gets out of the car, he greets the doorman with a "Hi, Eddy" and gives him a hug. At breakfast the next morning, Rachel spills her juice. Henry responds, "That's okay, I do it all the time."

When Henry goes to the library with Rachel, he flips paper wads at her because he can't read. So Rachel teaches him. But what she can't teach him is how to become his old self at his law firm. His partners want everything to return to the way it was before the shooting. However, going back to the past is impossible for Henry. He is a different man. His focus has turned to others rather than himself. He wants to reopen the hospital case; he doesn't want Rachel to leave to attend a school she has no desire for; he holds hands with and shows public affection for Sarah. He is aware of and cares for the people closest to him in life. He asks lots of questions. Henry values the time he can spend with a daughter he is just beginning to know.

Regarding Henry paints a vivid picture of what it means to put others first. If we look around us, we can discover it is modeled by many people who haven't had a bullet wound to the head. Sometimes it takes a catastrophic situation for us to change or for a spiritual decision to head in a different direction.

Putting others first is expressed in the following six character traits:

#1: We Desire to Share

True generosity makes people pause and acknowledge that a divine act has occurred. Such people practice selfless giving of time or energy unexpectedly and in undeserved quantities. Sometimes money is the vehicle for expression of generosity.

When we give to a friend, we express love and appreciation. But when we give to those who can't return the favor, our giving reaches godly stature. Sometimes people give out of duty or obligation, doing what is expected. Giving from compassion establishes true charity.

The Florida Fellowship Foundation, a fund that gives anonymously to people in need, is an example of this type of generosity. The men who established the fund recalled the popular television show from the late 1950s called *The Millionaire*. Each week on the show an unsuspecting person with an overwhelming situation was visited by a representative of a wealthy benefactor. Then the person was given a check for one million dollars. Watching their joy and expressions of gratitude was overwhelming. While the Florida Fellowship Foundation doesn't give away a million dollars, it does meet needs that are brought to its attention. Sometimes a car is beyond repair with no means to purchase another, or a medical operation depletes family resources. Helping people provides its own reward: a personal sense of satisfaction in having the resources to assist worthy people or causes.

When people give from their meagerness, heaven is alerted. Some of the most generous people on earth are not the wealthiest. Visit a poor foreign country, and you will find Christians sharing literally everything they own with those in need. And they do it joyfully. Church services in these countries are exhibitions of praise as the people whom we would consider to be desperately needy sing chorus after chorus at full volume. Visit their homes, and many of them will prepare for their guest elaborate meals far beyond their means. By comparison, their generosity makes our own seem insignificant.

#2: We Realize We Are Interconnected

It's easy to adopt a "Lone Ranger" mentality, especially since the American ideal of rugged individualism is promoted as the colonial ideal that developed the New World. I'll grant that it took tremendous courage, fortitude, and resourcefulness to survive in the untamed wilderness. But no colonialist would have survived without community.

The New Testament makes it clear that spiritual survival is dependent on caring for one another. As the apostle Paul established churches throughout Asia and Macedonia, he built their foundation on intimate and vulnerable relationships. Paul knew that community was critical for these new churches to survive. The term *one another* appears constantly throughout the Epistles, giving us examples of what it's like to be an interconnected Christian:

- They are devoted to one another (Romans 12:10).
- They give preference to one another (Romans 12:10).
- They are of the same mind toward one another (Romans 12:16).
- They love one another (Romans 13:8).
- They refrain from judging one another (Romans 14:13).
- They edify one another (Romans 14:19).
- They work for unity (Romans 15:5).
- They instruct one another (Romans 15:14).
- They serve one another (Galatians 5:13).
- They don't hurt one another (Galatians 5:15).
- They don't provoke one another through conceit (Galatians 5:26).
- They help carry one another's burdens (Galatians 6:2).
- They are patient with one another (Ephesians 4:2).
- They are kind and forgive one another (Ephesians 4:32).
- They submit to one another (Ephesians 5:21).
- They esteem one another (Philippians 2:3).
- They don't deceive one another (Colossians 3:9).
- They encourage one another (1 Thessalonians 4:18).

- They stimulate one another to good works (Hebrews 10:24).
- They don't slander one another (James 4:11).
- They don't complain against one another (James 5:9).
- They confess their sins to one another (James 5:16).
- They pray for one another (James 5:16).
- They extend hospitality to one another (1 Peter 4:9).

These amazing principles apply to sports, business, or the church. Once Lee Iacocca asked the legendary football coach Vince Lombardi to share his formula for success. Lombardi responded, "You have to start by teaching the fundamentals. . . . Next, you've got to keep them in line. That's discipline. The men have to play as a team, not as a bunch of individuals. There's no room for prima donnas. But there have been a lot of coaches with good ball clubs who know the fundamentals and have plenty of discipline but still don't win the game. Then you come to the third ingredient: If you're going to play together as a team, you've got to care for one another. You've got to love each other. . . . The difference between mediocrity and greatness is the feeling these guys have for each other."

Two thousand years ago Paul knew prima donnas destroy team spirit. Perhaps unknowingly, the Lombardis and Iacoccas of the world have adopted biblical principles to achieve national success.

#3: We Are Respectful, Courteous, and Affirming

The dictionary defines *courtesy* as "gracious politeness . . . a considerate act or remark." One marriage counselor believes 80 percent of the coldness and estrangements of married life is due to the lack of courtesy on the part of the husband or wife.

My friend Bill constantly looks for ways to encourage and affirm me. Several times when I've had to preach at the funerals of close friends, Bill calls to let me know he is concerned and praying. Bill also has provided funds for my children's college education, and I know he has done the same for others. He lifts the load for people wherever he can.

When people like Bill put others first, they constantly look for ways to affirm those who are closest to them. The old saying "Charity begins at home" could also read "Affirmation begins at home." The ego of every child is either pumped up or deflated by the words of his parents. When children don't receive kind words from parents, they grow up to be adults who still desperately search for affirmation.

One reconnaissance pilot had a successful career in the air force and was given the responsibility to fly the lead position. After leaving the military, he became a pilot for Delta Air Lines. One morning, just before the plane was airborne, one of the two engines quit. His hours of simulator training paid off; he accomplished the difficult maneuver to get the plane off the ground.

Praised as a hero, he received letters of commendation from the passengers, the president of Delta, and from old air force buddies who heard what happened.

Several days later he heard from his dad, a retired air force fighter pilot. Jokingly the father said, "Well, if you hadn't had your foot on the brake, you wouldn't have had the problem." The joke fell flat and became painful words for the son. It reminded him of the missing words he longed to hear from his dad: "Great job, Son."

The committed Christian, if centered on others, freely gives polite affirmation to others.

#4: We Are Available

When a tragedy strikes, a person doesn't need to hear platitudes or a Scripture verse. Words such as "I know how you feel" don't mean much. Instead, this person needs the quiet presence of a friend. Friends with an orientation to others make themselves available on these occasions.

When I was fifteen, my eight-year-old brother, Don, lost control while riding his bike next to a moving concrete truck. He was killed instantly.

Only a few months earlier our family had moved to Cheyenne, Wyoming. I had met a wonderful group of friends who were committed Christians. Their faith was so infectious and vital that I wanted what they had. So the week before Don's death, I committed my life to Christ.

After the accident, one of those friends, Gary, spent hours with me. He had a spiritual maturity that far exceeded his fifteen years. He said or did very little. He was just there, and that's what I needed. Although my brother died thirty years ago, I still remember Gary's act of selflessness as if it happened just yesterday.

Few people know about the profound spiritual influence that a Quaker widow, Eliza Gurney, had on President Abraham Lincoln. October 26, 1862, marked a dark time in American history. The Civil War was raging, and victory could have gone either direction. President Lincoln agreed to meet with Eliza Gurney and a few friends. He thought it was for an interview since her husband, Joseph John Gurney, had been a famous English banker and Quaker minister.

But Eliza and her friends called on the president for no other reason than to give spiritual support. They wanted to be available to a president deeply wounded by sorrow. Their fifteen-minute interview was extended much longer.

After the meeting those present described it as "the most awful silence." The president was accustomed to hearing speeches and advice on what steps he ought to take to win the war. What he wasn't accustomed to was group silence. Tears ran down his cheeks.

When the time was right, Eliza gave a short sermon, then

knelt to offer a short but comprehensive prayer. She asked that the president receive light and wisdom. Following further silence, Lincoln summarized thoughts that had been developing for more than a year of intellectual and spiritual struggle. It was a remarkably insightful view of the spiritual nature of his struggle in the War between the States. He believed he was an instrument in the hands of a sovereign God to preserve the Union.

Lincoln maintained correspondence with Eliza because she had followed the inner call to be available. Almost two years later, Lincoln wrote, "I have not forgotten—probably never shall forget—the very impressive occasion when yourself and friends visited me on a Sabbath forenoon two years ago."

President Lincoln desperately needed spiritual support and found it in a person who gave without a trace of self-seeking.[1]

#5: We Enjoy Other People's Success

One of the greatest stories about friendship in the Bible is that of King Saul's son Jonathan and the shepherd boy David. Though Saul had been chosen by God to be the king, he eventually disqualified himself through his selective obedience and became consumed with envy toward God's anointed replacement, David. On several occasions, Saul tried to pin David against the wall with his spear, but to no avail. Without an insider who knew of Saul's intentions, David couldn't have survived. Jonathan risked his own life to help David escape.

Sometimes I wonder if Jonathan ever pondered who the next king would be. If so, David would have been a competitor to Jonathan. But, according to the Bible, no one wanted David to succeed more than his friend Jonathan. Competition was not a factor in their strong bond of friendship.

It's impossible to enjoy the success of anyone when you feel competitive. People who put others first are also self-assured. They aren't threatened when those closest to them receive recognition or applause. They can stand and give the ovation and return to the tasks they know they are suited for. These committed Christians choose not to lose sleep over medals, skyrocketing career paths, or financial portfolios of others. Because greed and envy have been disarmed, they make their own significant contribution to the world.

#6: We Protect Others from Social Embarrassment

Each story Jesus shared had several layers of interpretation. For instance, there is double meaning in Jesus' story of turning water into wine at a Galilean wedding. The story is truly about Jesus' first miracle: the supernatural aspect of transforming water to wine. But it is also about a mother who understands the social embarrassment for the bride and groom. They had underestimated the amount of refreshments needed for the biggest event of their lives. The Scriptures don't give a wealth of information about Mary, but we know that she put others first. She was willing to do anything she could to protect others from being socially embarrassed.

My administrative assistant, Anne Davis, is good at protecting me from social embarrassment. Whether it's a foundation letter or a contract, when she puts the material together, she asks, "Larry, have you thought about . . . ?" If I have, I'll tell her the reason. But there are times when she has saved me from misinterpretation by asking thoughtful questions.

How Do We Learn to Put Others First?

If you wish to learn how to put others first, you may find the following five steps helpful:

Step #1: Identify Strongholds of Selfishness

List ways you express selfishness. Maybe you don't do your share of the housework. Or you don't give your job or your family your full attention or your best expertise. Or you are always on the receiving end of concern or gifts, rather than giving of yourself to others in friendship.

Step #2: Attack One Giant at a Time

Plan active steps to bring down your strongholds of selfishness, one at a time. For instance, if you have been on the receiving end of a lopsided friendship, lay out a strategy to nourish your relationships. Take others out for lunch. Remember birthdays or other special occasions. Call and check up on friends. Discover their special interests, then surprise them with an appropriate gift. After you are on track and donating to your friends, turn to other giants of selfishness in your life and plan a similar course of attack.

Step #3: Find a Need and Fill It

Consider your church or people who are involved in various ministries. Possibly you've heard of someone who is struggling. Would a visit from you provide relief and encouragement? Consider an appropriate financial contribution to either an individual or a cause. Open your home to others. Write a letter. Cook a meal. Give young parents a night out by taking care of their children. Donate to a scholarship fund for students who can't afford college payments. As you begin to consider these things, you will be overwhelmed with the opportunities for selfless giving.

Step #4: Acquire an Attitude of Gratitude

Be creative. Think of the many opportunities you have to say thank you for little jobs well done. Compliment a meal. Tell a child you are proud of her. Help a coworker unload her car after buying office supplies. Return phone calls. Open the door for others. Offer your seat on the bus. Congratulate a soloist for an excellent performance. Acknowledge the accomplishments of your friends.

Step #5: Protect the Embarrassed

When you hear titillating gossip, stop before you share it. Instead, point out a mistake to a coworker before his supervisor finds out. Quietly warn a person who is about to commit a faux pas. Look for ways to provide an escape for those in an embarrassing situation.

The Bottom Line
The change won't happen overnight. If you try to accomplish too much at once, you will burn out quickly. But you can begin with a deliberate intent to focus on others and to do so step-by-step. Over time, acts will become habits, and habits will lead to change in character—the character of a godly, committed Christian.

THINKING IT THROUGH
1. Describe a time when you felt competitive. How did your competitive spirit interfere with centering on others?

2. What irritates you the most about self-absorbed people? Have you ever been self-absorbed? If so, what was the result in your life and in others' lives?

3. Have you had any experience with a self-centered Christian leader? If so, what offends you about that person? (Don't name names; just describe the situation and how it affected you and others.)

4. Look up the following verses. What do they have to say about putting others first?

- Psalm 37:25-26
- Romans 12:10
- 1 Corinthians 12:25
- 1 Corinthians 13:1-3
- 2 Corinthians 2:12-13
- Galatians 5:26

- Hebrews 13:1-3
- James 2:15-16

5. Describe a situation when someone was available for you when you needed him or her. How did that make you feel?

6. Who needs your attention right now? What can you do to focus on that person this week?

4

Take Risks

Life is a constant game of "double or nothing." We are always tempted to save what we have by refusing to put it at risk again. But this means the end of adventure.

PAUL TOURNIER

WHEN my two children, Brett and Erica, were in grade school, Susan and I packed them into our big blue LeSabre and headed for what is considered to be the single most dramatic mountain scene in the U.S.—the Grand Tetons.

I grew up in the wide open spaces of Wyoming. During one college summer, I worked for the Wyoming Highway Department, traveling the entire state and soaking in the beauty. Now I wanted to share the rugged mountains and crystal-clear trout streams with my family.

With trail map in hand and a lunch in our backpack, we took a boat ride across Jenny Lake. Our goal was to reach the first available snow. Then we hiked to a rushing waterfall and found a cool place near the mist to eat our lunch.

After lunch, a number of chipmunks scampered close by, pausing as if begging for leftover lunch scraps. "Oh, look at the hungry little things," we said, as we delightfully tossed a few crumbs their way.

While we were serving the chipmunks lunch, a ranger entered our dining area. "Folks, please don't feed the chipmunks," he said. "The posted signs about feeding the animals are there for a reason. If the animals become too comfortable with begging for handouts from tourists, there is a danger they will not forage for themselves. These chipmunks need to save for winter and have the proper nutrition to build a winter coat that will withstand the long cold months when their food is not available."

The ranger was right. We had been taking pleasure in feeding the chipmunks, but we hadn't stopped to think about the long-range effects of our welfare program.

What Is Comfort to You?

Since that incident, I've often thought about how we also gravitate to whatever comfort is available, even at the risk of losing our ability to experiment, to take risks, or accept new challenges.

Creature comforts are real, but they vary according to each person. Understanding what prevents us from taking risks will help us to move out of our comfort zone physically, socially, mentally or emotionally, and spiritually.

Physical Comfort

Home sweet home. How we love the familiar! The sights, aromas, and memories are not only comfortable, they provide a sense of security. Everyone has special tastes that only local cuisine can satisfy. If you've lived in Texas, no other place can match the pecan-smoked barbecue or the Tex-Mex restaurants with fresh ingredients. The Mexican clones found in northern climates pale in comparison.

We become comfortable with local shopping areas; we know which stores offer particular products. Entertainment and sports options can quickly spoil us. Maybe we prefer to deep-sea fish in the Pacific or ski in the Rockies.

We also become comfortable with the noise of life. How difficult would it be to leave behind your radio, television, or Walkman and pursue quiet, even for a short time?

All of us are entrenched in the hooks of the familiar. And although familiar things are good in and of themselves, they can also keep us from seeking new experiences.

When I worked with Youth for Christ in Houston, I used to take busloads of high school students to the Colorado Rockies for summer camp. These students had a week of high adventure as they shot the rapids of the South Platte River in rubber life rafts or as they rappelled cliffs. Each evening the programs were jammed with skits and music, followed by stirring messages from some of the best youth communicators in the country.

Thursdays, however, were special. A mandatory discipline of silence followed the evening session. For one hour, students had to find a place to be completely alone. We encouraged them to pray or evaluate their life—even sleep if they wanted. The only requirement was silence.

With their colorful sweaters and blue-jean attire, the students scattered. A few climbed trees for the hour. Others sat on a car hood or a boulder. About thirty to forty-five minutes into the hour, things began to change. Some of the students began to fidget and get nervous.

A bell signaled the end of the hour. Everyone assembled at

71

the chapel. Some of the kids were shaking and wild-eyed as they returned. They looked like junkies waiting for their next fix of sound. Others cried, not able to handle the pain of silence or the emptiness of their own thoughts. Each student was reflective. Staff and students alike were looking for a stretching experience, and they found it in silence. But when the silence was over, they returned to the comfort of the familiar as quickly as possible.

When we leave our physical comfort zone, God can speak to us in the midst of that discomfort. He will help us become more reflective and open to his leading.

Social Comfort

Few of us accept the risk of leaving old friends and making new relationships. Building relationships takes time. If you have ever moved to a new community, you know how difficult it is to break into the existing social order. This is especially true for an adult if you don't have children or your children are grown. Children lead the way and give you common ground for new social relationships, such as Little League games, tennis matches, dance recitals, or church activities.

The familiar is so comfortable socially that it's easy to understand why people want to be around their already established friends. For many, these friends are a prerequisite for happiness.

At a club near my workplace, the same twelve men gather each day for lunch. Laughter and good conversation fill the air during the meal. If someone doesn't attend for several days, the men want to know why. From a positive perspective, they experience the security of place and belonging. But on the other hand, there is the tendency to become cliquish. There is no need to meet new friends, and the relationships can become stale. Each man has heard the same stories told and expanded a hundred times over.

To reach out to a new circle of friends, we need a deliberate plan of action, personal courage, and a willingness to face possible rejection in light of the lives we can touch.

Mental Comfort

Media largely shapes our mind and culture. As Harry Blamires says, "Modern mass media are forming not only mentalities but total personalities on a vast scale. It is not just that we are being seduced by advertisers to buy X's chocolate instead of Y's. We, or our fellowmen, are being conditioned by advertisers to believe that such and such things constitute the fullness of life."[1]

Everyone gets locked into certain patterns of thinking. It's uncomfortable for us to change. And it's difficult for us mentally to challenge popular thinking generated by the press, politicians, clergy, or our peers. We may think it's impolite to do so. So we refrain from expressing an opposing view.

However, by being reluctant to risk involvement in dialogue, Christians can miss the opportunity for new understanding and awareness. Are we turned off by watching heated debates and arguments on television talk shows? While these kinds of programs are more for entertainment than actual debate, we can be challenged by the various intellectual viewpoints.

To risk leaving our mental comfort zone, we have to be willing to take time to read from a wide spectrum of material. (We'll discuss this further in the chapter on diligent study.) In our reading, we may begin asking questions, such as, Are my presuppositions about life wrong? Are there holes in my theological framework? Are my ethics overly culturized? Are my politics overly materialistic? Is my scientific understanding religiously biased?

Some Christians, for instance, are so paranoid they won't even begin to read about the debate between evolution and seven-day creationists. They are worried that through science or astronomy they will learn something that contradicts their biblical beliefs. Many are afraid that if one component is shattered, they'll have to throw out their entire worldview. Most often, serious study results in the opposite. Turning to science validates the Scriptures and is intellectually stretching. Jay Kesler used to say, "God doesn't have sweaty palms that people are going to find out about him something that he doesn't want them to know."

It is safer to retreat to the familiar instead of facing risks. Sometimes it is easier to pick up the mental television channel changer and let the professors deal with issues like evolution. But committed Christians want to be challenged intellectually.

Spiritual Comfort

If you are a Christ follower, do you remember the excitement and hunger you had when you first came to know Christ? The Bible came alive with insights, and you spent hours soaking up the stories. How long did it take for you to be comfortable in your growth pattern?

Many people soon find it difficult to try different churches or to change their thoughts about discipleship or their strategy for evangelism. Their limited experience colors their ideas. At first, growth comes quickly. They can't get enough biblical understanding. They discover spiritual gifts and gratifying worship experiences. But it isn't long before they learn that leaders aren't gods who know everything but humans who are sometimes self-centered. At this point, new Christians may decide to eat their spiritual food cafeteria style—picking and choosing along the way. After this experimentation, they acquire a taste for a specific style of preaching, liturgy, church size, and government.

Before long, they settle into a routine. Spiritual life falls into a boring rut. Different speakers use the same illustrations, and the audience becomes overly familiar with the interpretation of certain passages. Gems from the Bible no longer pop up whenever they open their Bibles. Now it takes months of mining to uncover unique truths. Unfortunately, many of these Christians advance to the next stage where they lower their standards of expectations. "Our kids need the church," they say, but what they leave unspoken is their willingness to accept the staleness of predictability.

When we lived in Houston, I learned that one of my college friends lived in the same town. Although my family and I tried to get together with her, she was unavailable. Her particular church believed that each person should receive instruction from only one pastor and required that everyone attend Bible study every single night of the week. The people who attended quickly fell into a mind-set of unquestioned loyalty. While comfortable, they were limited in their spiritual growth—not to mention their social horizons.

Venturing away from spiritually comfortable territory creates multiple problems. We may have to answer questions from family, friends, and the clergy. We may hurt people's feelings. But spiritual life can only be revived by being adventurous.

Wired for Adventure!
Ralph Veerman has had great success helping parachurch organizations, such as Youth for Christ, Prison Fellowship, and Ligonier Ministries. Until a few years ago, he had always functioned on the inside of the organization. Then he had the desire to start his own business. It was a risk, and he sought godly counsel for his feelings of uncertainty. But since starting his own consulting business to parachurch organizations, Veerman's business has grown rapidly. He began with a strong sense of adventure and moved out of his comfort zone.

These days many people are touting the term *burnout.*

Psychologists say that burnout isn't the result of overwork but the by-product of unproductive work. How many people do you know who enjoy their work? Many go to their jobs day after day and just punch the clock. When someone has a skill and the desire and ability to express himself, and yet refuses to use that gift, he feels guilt. If this person is overworked in his present job, it's likely that he'll burn out.

But adventure is healthy; it's the way we're wired. Animals are impelled through life by instinct and couldn't care less about self-expression. However, humans have desires and longings that either are or are not fulfilled.

For children, every day is a new discovery. Likewise, adults cannot express themselves without being creative in some area. However, adults have enough mileage to know that sometimes their expressions of creativity are not appreciated. Sometimes they fail, and it's more comfortable to stop and not risk visiting that pain again.

Our Adventurous, Creative God

Paul Tournier, a Swiss psychologist and devout Christian, has described the innovative nature of God. God is adventurous, a fact that is seen in the variety of his creative expressions. Study one aspect of creation—like the variety found in the animal kingdom—and you will quickly be overwhelmed by thousands of species. God has invented numerous solutions to the technical difficulties of his creation. For instance, flying can be accomplished either via feathers, as with a bird, or without feathers, as with the bat. Insects fly by means of a multitude of various membranes. God didn't create claws and then stop. There are hooves and fingernails. He made everything unique and is our greatest example of imagination.

Many of us try to pattern ourselves after someone else. But exact imitation is impossible and even violates God's intent. That's why we need to continually yield control of our lives to

God. Then he can make us originals. As an original, you can keep growing, keep learning, and keep moving (even when it is uncomfortable). You can keep uniquely expressing yourself.

Adventurous Role Models of the Bible

There are many examples in the Bible of creative, adventurous people who chose to walk with God, even in uncomfortable situations.

In Exodus 1, the Egyptian pharaoh gave an order that all newborn Jewish boys be killed. Instead, the Hebrew midwives lied to Pharaoh about sparing the newborn males.

In Joshua 2, Jewish spies were sent into the Promised Land. When Rahab, a prostitute, hid those two spies in Jericho and lied about their whereabouts, she chose adventure with God.

In 1 Samuel 19, Michal, David's wife and Saul's daughter, deceived her father's messengers. They were pursuing David, so Michal put a dummy in bed and informed Saul's soldiers that David was ill. In the meantime, he had the opportunity to escape.

Throughout these stories and in the rest of the Bible, nothing is said about the moral nature of these actions. But it seems that God applauds the creativity of these people especially when someone's life was at stake—especially during times of war. In the midst of overwhelming circumstances, they became innovative. In each case, the innovation was toward God's pleasure. Rahab saved the lives of the spies; the midwives saved newborn males, including Moses; and Michal saved David's life and prevented her father from committing murder.

God promotes this type of resourcefulness. Since we are created in his image, God is pleased to see us take the creative road—not just the safe road. It's true that the creative road contains many dangerous turns and unavoidable potholes.

But if we quit and refuse to leave the comfort of safety, we deny our created nature, our uniqueness, and we slowly die.

But What about Failure?

No one enjoys failing. For some people, the potential of failure shackles them into inactivity. But few people succeed without facing their fear of failure. In athletics, business, or the church, the joy of success comes with knowing the realities of failure.

We Are Already Successful in God's Eyes

For years, we may have heard through sermons that "God doesn't want our ability; he wants our availability" or "God doesn't call us to be successful, but to be faithful." While there is truth in those statements, the Bible also promotes ability and success. After all, in the final scope of events, God is sovereign. He wins—in spite of our setbacks. Many of these setbacks may not be overcome in our lifetime, but they will be, in heaven.

The Bible is filled with the language of success:

> The Lord was with Joseph and gave him success in whatever he did. *Genesis 39:23*

> In everything [David] did he had great success, because the Lord was with him. *1 Samuel 18:14*

> [David to his son Solomon:] Then you will have success if you are careful to observe the decrees and laws that the Lord gave Moses for Israel. *1 Chronicles 22:13*

> As long as [Uzziah] sought the Lord, God gave him success. *2 Chronicles 26:5*

> May he give you the desire of your heart and make all your plans succeed. *Psalm 20:4*

> Plans fail for lack of counsel, but with many advisers they succeed. *Proverbs 15:22*

> Commit to the Lord whatever you do, and your plans will succeed. *Proverbs 16:3*

The bottom line is this: God's plans, combined with our actions, guarantee success. That success may not be earthly success, but it will always be heavenly success. The fear of failure is meaningless if God is involved. We need to commit our works to him and get on with it. The timing for success is totally unpredictable, so we should leave these issues in God's hands. God can handle the calendar.

But take this caution to heart: The more success you attain, the greater the appetite for slaying larger giants. Smaller victories will never satisfy you again. This lack of satisfaction will be a thorn in the flesh to remind you that all attainments in this life are shallow compared to what awaits us when we get to heaven.

We Are Overcomers

Most people want to overcome the fear of failure and are looking for a guarantee. Take my friend Jim, for instance. An airline pilot, Jim still had ten years before retirement. He was concerned about the financial shape of his company; it was uncertain they would last another six months. As I visited with him at his beautiful hillside home, he asked, "What does a fifty-year-old ex-pilot do for a living if he can't fly?"

As we took a stroll, I told him about talking to scores of men who had faced similar situations. In every case, they were scared to death. "I don't know a single man who didn't ultimately rebound," I told Jim. "Sure, there were struggles. Some changed locations. Others sold their homes. But each one landed on his feet. Psalm 37:25 says, 'I was young and now I am old, yet I have never seen the righteous forsaken or their children begging bread.' Now, Jim, remember that David's viewpoint was limited. He couldn't observe all people in all places of the world for all time. He's not saying no one ever went hungry—he experienced such pangs himself. But, as a general principle, he is saying God provides for his own, either through opportunities he makes available or through help from others.

"The psalmist understood that difficult circumstances make success seem like an illusion. But when we face sorrow, the Lord's discipline, or persecution for our faith, we can say with the psalmist, 'He who dwells in the shelter of the Most High will rest in the shadow of the Almighty.'"

At this point, people usually want to throw a "how about" illustration into the conversation. What about my Christian friend George, who lost his business then died of cancer? How about Dietrich Bonhoeffer, the famous Lutheran theologian who confronted Hitler at great personal risk and paid for it with his life? Or Eric Liddell, the runner portrayed in *Chariots of Fire,* who later wasted away and died in a Chinese prison camp? Bonhoeffer and Liddell moved beyond their comfort zones. They stood up to fear and did what they could, when they could, and with all of the ingenuity they could muster. Success for these men came after their deaths, when they made an impact larger than they could ever dream. If God is in it, then it survives—whether it is recognized by the public or something private in the lives of our children.

Paul Tournier describes a vicious cycle of failure that catches those who refuse to leave their comfort zone. Anxiety engenders fear; fear paralyzes and then breaks the spirit. The cycle saps the joy from life and results in self-centeredness. Self-centered people turn from adventure because they can't risk failure.

Jim, my airline pilot friend, took many risks. Since he is incredibly competent, his skills eventually reduced his risks. The fears were real, but Jim is succeeding because he isn't paralyzed or self-centered. He will keep moving ahead because he believes in carrying out God's plan for his life, no matter how unsure he feels about himself.

We Have True Security

Years ago, I had a life-insurance policy I thought was secure. I enjoyed the high yields it provided on my cash values. However, when the company failed and had to be temporarily rescued by the state, millions of dollars in policies, including mine, were tied up in the courts for years. Eventually another company purchased the policies and everything was resolved. But my security in insurance evaporated.

Some are looking for security in the Social Security system. Our government is trying to provide security through programs like Medicare or universal health-care coverage. Although without these entitlements many people cannot survive, the programs also serve to make the larger population dependent on and accustomed to these hand-fed provisions. In a sense, we become like the chipmunk in the opening pages of this chapter. We can't forage for ourselves and survive the cold winters.

Some people are content with predictable lives and aren't attracted to adventure. Even adventurists want some elements of security and stability—especially when they have a spouse and children who depend on a stable income.

It's okay to want both. God is the God of creativity and also the God who said, "I change not." His attributes never change because God cannot change who he is. One of God's attributes is creativity, and he is predictable when he works creatively with us. If we are attracted solely to security and predictability, then we deny the creative characteristics we have inherited from God. We also set ourselves up for a rude awakening, because apart from God there is no such thing as security.

Society will try to convince us that we can have security. There is life insurance, health insurance, disability insurance, homeowner's insurance, liability insurance, director's and officer's insurance, medical insurance, and so on. Although creative adventurists want to be covered just like everyone else, they don't let that search for security keep them from stepping out to take risks.

How can we have both security and innovation? By moving out with God and letting him guide us. If we hesitate to move out into something different, our vision will be blurred, creating even greater confusion and anxiety. Security will always elude those who don't take risks because our security comes ultimately from a God who is on the move. Without him, all forms of security disappear like vapor.

Moving out of Your Comfort Zone

Moving out of your comfort zone means different things at various stages of life. The toddler toddles because he is attempting to walk. The grade school child tries to play the piano or baseball. The high school student competes scholastically and tests various relationships. The college student experiments with disciplines of study or tries to prepare for a career. Young adults risk loving and being loved and then approaching the adventures of marriage and parenthood. New careers are testing grounds for ideas, but then there is a new dimension—investments, retirement, and the search for security in the future.

For some, it screeches to a halt. They don't want any more experiments. They are locked in—physically, socially, mentally, and maybe even spiritually—and the light begins to dim in their eyes. But this isn't the way God wants us to experience his best for us.

The Bible's "Faith Hall of Fame"

Hebrews 11, the "Faith Hall of Fame," introduces us to a lineup of people who left their comfort zones:

> Abel offered a better sacrifice than Cain.
> Noah built a boat without knowing about floods.
> Abraham left the security of Ur for the promise of reward.
> Abraham's sons continued the journey.
> Moses' parents risked the anger of Pharaoh to protect him.
> Moses left the security of Egypt for the wilderness.

The same characteristic is in the words that Jesus uttered in the great commission: "Therefore go and make disciples of all nations" (Matthew 28:19). A committed Christian uses the word *go*. He knows that standing still in his personal growth will not bring contentment.

Jesus Christ shared the same creative dynamics as the Father. He modeled adventure. Just examine his style of communication. It isn't pinpointed in one style but takes many forms. He addressed large crowds, then fed them. He touched those he healed, at least part of the time; with others Jesus spat on some dirt. Walking into the temple, Jesus overturned traders' tables and taught about merchandising. When he was taken captive by Roman soldiers, Jesus didn't say a word to his accusers.

Jesus did the unexpected. He appeared in unexpected places like a manger, or walking on a lake, or eating with sinners. His emotions ranged from tender to resolute to patient to sometimes indignant. He could discuss theology, farming, economics, or politics. While Jesus was controversial, he didn't grandstand. The Lord was constantly on the move, not restricted by or avoiding any family responsibilities.

Jesus talked about leaving and venturing. He told us to be salt to a world that needs savoring or light to a dark world. Jesus stood with courage against the religious leaders of his day and told us to leave behind our archaic views of the law, the posturing of religious exhibitionists, and our anxiety-driven fears about security or preconceived ways that God works. According to Jesus, we should venture out with news that heals physically and spiritually. We should leave social and cultural discriminations behind, along with relatives who try to restrict us from enlarging the boundaries of our expression. And we should be reintroduced to the simplicity of trust and the wonder of discovery that children have.

Risk taking is uncomfortable. But it can be rewarding. The woman I met in my adult Sunday school class is just one example.

Portrait of a Woman Who Moved beyond Her Comfort Zone

As I was about to conclude a lesson one Sunday, a lady whom I didn't know raised her hand and asked to say something to the class. For a split second, I thought, *This could be dangerous or even embarrassing. How do I graciously turn her down?* From experience, I knew that people sometimes say unusual things, but this woman didn't appear agitated. Though calm, she looked as if she didn't feel very well.

"What do you want to say?" I asked.

"I'll only take a minute," she said as she stood. "I want to ask the class to take care of my fiancé." She pointed to the man next to her.

"It's about time to dismiss, but briefly tell us what's on your mind." I stepped away from the podium but didn't sit down so I could quickly intercept if necessary. The class was deathly quiet. If any had been dozing during the lesson, they were now wide awake.

Slowly, but articulately, she began. "My name is Kristeen, and I've only a couple of weeks to live. I'm Jewish, and I have a form of leukemia, AML, that is particular to Jewish people. I'm going to die, and I'm all right with that, but Bob is really struggling and needs your prayers and support. I'm asking that you be here for him after I am gone."

She paused for a moment and I asked, "Kristeen, could we pray for you?"

At first she hesitated, then answered, "No, really, I'm at peace with what's going to happen to me. I'm not trying to focus attention on me, but on Bob."

I continued, "If you don't mind, we have several elders in this class, and we would like to be faithful to our responsibility. There's no guarantee of healing, but we would like to pray for you if you are willing." She agreed, but I could tell she was not totally comfortable with the attention I was giving her. Four elders came to the front, and we laid hands on Kristeen as I prayed.

After my prayer, I sensed nothing different. Kristeen still looked drawn and weak. After the class, several of the class members, including my wife, Susan, began asking her questions. They learned her first husband, a medic in Vietnam, had been killed in a helicopter crash. He had been trying to return home after having learned that Kristeen had given birth to a severely deformed daughter. Years later this daughter had come to Christ in the permanent-care facility where she had lived. At first, Kristeen had been outraged that her Jewish daughter, the granddaughter of an orthodox rabbi (who was also a survivor of a German concentration camp) had become a Christian without her permission. However, this daughter's life and words eventually had led to Kristeen's own conversion.

Now Kristeen was dying. Her Jewish doctor had been a close friend of her deceased husband. Their last hope was to try genetic engineering. During the next two weeks, her condition worsened. One Sunday she decided to be baptized. Her condition was so weak it was doubtful she could make it through the service. Jim, the associate pastor, had taken a special interest in Kristeen. He cupped his hand and gently laid the water on her head as he prayed for her spiritual and physical welfare. As the water touched her head, Kristeen felt an intense heat go through her body. She can't remember any specifics about the service, but she knew God had touched her. Today Kristeen and Bob are married, and there is no sign of the AML.

Kristeen captured the sense of adventure and creativity of God. She ventured out and told her story to a group of strangers in a Presbyterian church. We then moved out of our comfort zone in the class and responded in a similar spirit. We laid hands on her for healing—not the typical *modus operandi* for our denomination.

Sometimes we will do and say things that will cause people to question our spiritual balance. In those circumstances, we can get our comfort from the characters in the Bible. From Abraham to the apostles, we have vivid examples of those who moved out (despite their uncomfortable feelings at the moment) and allowed God to do a new thing. This kind of spontaneity makes us—and the church—come alive.

However, spontaneity is not a license for irresponsible actions. Every spiritually responsible decision grows from a wealth of biblical understanding, sensible timing, respect for spiritual authority, and much prayer. It is an ongoing battle of the Christian life for believers to know when to act and when tradition or conformity dictates otherwise.

The Bottom Line

How do you move out of your comfort zone? Here are three suggestions for taking action and growing in this critical characteristic of a committed Christian.

It Takes a "Go" Attitude

In 1966 Susan and I were interns for Youth for Christ in Beirut, Lebanon. Studying the Arabic language each day was one thing, but trying to speak it conversationally on the street was another.

The language has subtle nuances of pronunciation, and I didn't want to embarrass myself in public. But I knew I wouldn't make any progress without risking making a fool of myself. So I ventured into a small hole-in-the-wall café where the customers were old men in robes and fezzes. They had come to drink coffee and smoke their water pipes. To my surprise, they were flattered that I tried speaking their language. Together we laughed as I attempted to roll my *r*s and cough up sounds from the back of my throat. Slowly and very hesitantly I began to communicate because I had a "go" mentality.

For thirty-three years, George Wilson worked in the data processing area of the guided missile division of the Martin Marietta Corporation. When he retired, Wilson started Missionary Computer Fellowship in the basement of the First Presbyterian Church in Orlando. Along with a number of other frustrated retired engineers and computer whizzes, George began gutting standard IBM-compatible computers and replacing the parts with industrial-strength components that could withstand the rigors of operation in the jungle. They converted the computers to run from a twelve-volt battery. Finally, they invited missionaries for training on how to use these computers in language translation. Today, because George took a risk and moved outside his comfort zone, a steady stream of missionaries around the globe are knocking years (and decades) off the process of translating the Bible.

It didn't stop there. This sixty-two-year-old man decided to go to the small Russian village of Stuping to be a lay pastor for three months until a Russian pastor was available. For years, Stuping was a secret city because two aerospace plants are located there. Now a retired American defense engineer, who had spent his life helping to create weapons to destroy Russia, was targeting a secret weapons city with the gospel of peace. George once said, "You spend thirty-three years at an aerospace plant, and you know what *useless* is." But George was not useless. He was not mentally restricted by either a frustrating career or two failed marriages. As a totally committed follower of Christ, he continued looking for the next adventure—going, doing, being whatever God had in mind. Today George lives near St. Petersburg and studies Russian full-time. I can still hear him say, "I've tasted the total-commitment cookie, and I can't put it down."

You also can have this experience if you choose to have a "go" attitude.

Remember the Past

Throughout the Bible, the stories about the exodus of Israel from Egypt and the people crossing the Red Sea are retold dozens of times. Why? Because God knows we have short memories. Also, these stories are an example of how God leads. Have you ever been in a situation without financial resources, and God provided for you? Don't forget it. Find a notebook and begin a journal with these stories. Then whenever you are tempted to quit or you are hesitant to take a step or face monumental objections to your dreams, remember. If you are discouraged, force yourself to remember. Then pray, thanking God for his actions in the past and asking him for new provisions in your current situation.

What Can You Gain?

Taste the total-commitment cookie. You will feel alive, important, and useful. Soon you will be an example to others who observe your life. Once a year, George Wilson comes home for a couple of months. He gives a report to the elders. And he gives the children's talk during the worship service, showing them souvenirs of Russia and telling them about life in another country. He also shares what it's like to leave the comforts of home to fulfill this adventure God has given him. The children hang on his every word. Perhaps someday they will go too—maybe not to Russia or to a foreign mission field, but to wherever God leads.

These children have a marvelous heritage of observing a man who is still dreaming dreams and still severing the tethers of safety and predictability in his seventh decade of life.

We all can leave our comfort zones and take a risk for the Lord. Then, step-by-step, we'll grow into living examples of what it means to follow Jesus Christ as committed Christians.

THINKING IT THROUGH

1. What comforts would be extremely hard for you to give up in order to take risks?

2. Describe a time when . . .

   • you took a risk and it paid off.
   • you took a risk and it didn't pay off.

3. What does security mean to you? Have the "secure things" in your life ever failed you? If so, what happened?

4. Read the following passages. What do they say about taking risks or leaving comfort zones?

   • Genesis 6:11-22
   • Genesis 12:1-4
   • Exodus 2:1-10
   • 2 Chronicles 26:5
   • Matthew 6:25-34
   • Luke 8:42b-48
   • Philippians 3:12-14
   • Hebrews 11:24-27

5. Think about the people you know. Are any of them models of taking risks? If so, who? And how have you seen them leave their comfort zones?

6. What can you do this week to step out of your comfort zone? Ask God to help you take that first risky step.

5

Study Diligently

More than any other single fact, [Cotton] Mather's practical success with inoculation established the idea that the smallpox might eventually be conquered, and this incidentally opened men's minds to the curability of other diseases. DANIEL J. BOORSTIN

PURITAN. The very word conjures up anger and hatred from many people toward these seventeenth- and eighteenth-century zealots because so many people equate puritanical thinking with sexual repression, witch-hunting, and legalism. However, people interested in serious scholarship have discovered some unlikely heroes in the American colonies. They were not only Puritans but Puritan preachers with insatiable appetites for philosophy, science, law, horticulture, medicine, and serious study. Cotton Mather (1663–1728) was one such pastor.

In the colonies and Europe, people were filled with fear when they heard the word *smallpox* because, other than quarantine, medical science had no way to treat the disease. Wealthy Americans, who could afford to send their sons to Europe for higher education, refused to do so because of this fear. Indians, in particular, were susceptible, and many tribes were nearly wiped out. More died from this disease than from musket wounds.

Cotton Mather had an overactive and practical mind. In fact, British scientists were so impressed with his gifts of observation that they awarded him an honorary degree from the University of Aberdeen and membership in the Royal Society. Along with the preparation of sermons, he studied and classified plants, birds, lightning, and Indian cures.

While reading a letter from a Turkish doctor in the publication *Transactions of the Royal Society of London 1714*, Mather discovered a possible way to save New England from smallpox: If a healthy person was deliberately infected with smallpox, it usually produced either a light case of the disease or the patient eventually recovered.

Smallpox became an epidemic throughout Boston in 1721, when a ship from the West Indies carried the disease as part of its cargo. Although Mather appealed to the physicians to try inoculation, most were angered at the idea. *Who does Cotton Mather think he is, suggesting we try an unfamiliar technique from reading the writings of a Muslim?* they wondered.

Public opinion mounted against Mather, and he was discredited in *The New England Courant*, which was founded by James Franklin, brother of Benjamin. The controversy intensified, and in November someone threw a bomb in Mather's house.

Then news arrived in Boston that the inoculations had been attempted in London and were highly successful. Since half of the people in Boston were ill with smallpox, there wasn't much to risk in trying inoculations. As Daniel J. Boorstin writes, "In March 1722, after the worst of the epidemic was over, Mather pointed out to the Secretary of the Royal Society in London that of nearly 300 inoculated in Boston only five or six had died (and perhaps these had already been naturally infected before their inoculation), while of the more than 5,000 who caught the disease naturally, nearly 900 had died."[1]

Before the next epidemic arrived from Ireland during 1729 and 1730, the Boston physicians needed no persuasion about the merits of inoculation. Eventually the rest of the colonies heard about their success. The physician-in-chief for George Washington convinced him to inoculate the entire army during the American Revolution. It was the most extensive medical experiment to be carried out in the new colonies.

We may not have the natural inquisitive gifts of Cotton Mather, but if we refuse to study, it indicates a lack of seriousness about the Christian faith. To impact society, a committed Christian needs to have a broad spectrum of knowledge, secular and scriptural. The problem is, many forces of modern society pull us away from the discipline of study. The big questions about life and its origin, about understanding our present circumstances in light of history, come only from diligent study—another key attribute for the committed Christian.

What competes for our attention and draws us away from study? First, a time crunch; second, a fuzzy cultural mind-set; and third, the constant bombardment of information that faces us every day.

Everyone Has a Time Crunch

Where does a businessperson, for example, find time for any kind of study during a typical day? The alarm sounds at 5:30 A.M. A microwaved breakfast is gobbled down on the way out the door. On the way to the office, a car phone is used to check in with the office answering machine. Then the person steps into the whirlwind of E-mail, faxes, and teleconferencing.

Appointments are crammed in, and the adrenaline flows into lunch. Squeezed into the schedule are some personal agendas, such as securing theater tickets, planning the next out-of-town business trip, and giving assistants next week's deadlines before rushing home to change clothes for a dinner appointment. Some people even attempt to work late at night on the laptop computer, only to have it crash. But our society has thought of everything. For the crashed computer, we can call the twenty-four-hour repair hotline. And the above example doesn't even include the time pressures of caring for children!

In the middle of this hurried lifestyle, everyone wants to appear intelligent. Recently I read a story about a rugged individual who entered a bookstore in greasy overalls. "How much would it cost to buy 128 feet of books?" he asked. The owner was caught by surprise and asked what the man had in mind. A group of trade-union leaders, hosting some educated associates, had hired this man because they were attempting to break a deadlock in volatile negotiations. They figured that the 128 feet of books would create the image of literary accomplishment and, when purchased by length on the shelf, would become a weapon of intimidation—even without being read.

Our Fuzzy Cultural Mind-Set

When C. S. Lewis wrote *The Screwtape Letters,* he included dialogue between a senior devil and a junior devil assigned to derail a person before that person slipped over to God's side.

"Go get him away from the Enemy," the senior devil demands. Sometime later the young imp returns, saying, "We lost him, he has gone all the way over to the Enemy's side."

"How did that happen?" the evil one inquires.

"Well," he answered, "he started to take a long walk every morning, just for the pleasure of it, and on these walks, the

Enemy became more audible to him. Further he read a good book, just for the pleasure of it, and the Enemy found him more receptive."

"That's where you blew it," says the senior devil. "If you had only had him walk for the sake of exercise, it would have become dreaded and tedious, devoid of pleasure. If you had only had him reading so he could parrot the contents to someone else, reading would become burdensome and boring rather than pleasurable. We could then have easily snared him."

Each of us uses imaginary glasses to see and evaluate the world around us. Unless we study and learn how to discriminate, it's like wearing sunglasses indoors and being unaware of the fact that our lenses are dark. For instance, believers may think they are seeing the world with a Christian mind-set, but instead they are evaluating everything from the world's point of view. If these believers serve on the boards of their churches, they may wrestle with issues such as how to appropriate money, how to get favorable decisions through committees or commissions, how to get pet projects on the agenda of session meetings, or even which carpet color should be used. There's nothing wrong with these issues. But are they the sum total of "Christian thought"? There are no Christian distinctions about such thoughts. Just because we spend time discussing the appropriation of funds for buildings and other projects in church meetings doesn't necessarily mean we have a Christian mind-set for these matters. Similar discussions could be held in any corporate boardroom. A Christian mind-set always considers the *why* behind such discussions and the spiritual effects and results of the expenses.

Let's say a Christian attorney is representing the defendant in a medical liability case. The attorney wrestles with the implications: Should believers attempt to gouge an insurance company just because the jury will go along with it? What are the long-term ramifications of such a decision on the public? By asking these questions, the attorney is looking at the world with a Christian mind-set. The attorney is evaluating the scope of life, in and out of the church, from God's perspective.

It's a Cultural Conflict

Practically every newspaper, television show, or movie is a reminder that the Christian viewpoint is in the minority. If Christians feel disappointed because the community doesn't embrace their philosophy or values, they're going to live in a funk for the rest of their lives. Here are three distinct areas of cultural difference:

First, today's society cannot accept absolute values. Although the erosion of absolute values has been happening for a long time, the skids were greased in the early seventies when values clarification hit public education. School administrators felt they could no longer advocate to a student what values were important. Students had to determine values for themselves. "Anything goes" was the message, and personal preference became the ultimate value. Values clarification didn't eliminate values. Rather, it opened young minds to the thoughts of sophisticated and creatively designed promoters, such as Hollywood.

When Hollywood slips its values in through television or movies, everyone becomes a victim—from adult to child, from teacher to student. But preferences and values change with the wind. One day a student might prefer situation ethics, free love, and a libertarian approach to government. The next day the same student may embrace a more structured approach to life. The subtle message is that nothing merits fidelity. If you are tired of a particular viewpoint or just plain bored, you can exchange it for a new one. Relationships fall into the same category. Sadly, many marriages have become expendable since there's no foundational value of commitment that endures.

Instead of clarifying our values and providing a new standard, the values clarification movement threw out the standard of the Bible and created greater confusion.

Second, people are eager for a multitude of experiences in an affluent society. At Universal Studios, we can experience *Back to the Future,* ride *Jaws,* and be a part of making *Murder She Wrote.* We can take adventure vacations or attend the Super Bowl or skydive or snorkel or visit the Louvre in Paris. There's nothing inherently wrong with any of these activities. The problem occurs when we fail to take time to evaluate whether the experience is worthwhile.

Amusement is the key word for our society, which tends to think, *While the experience is pleasurable, why ask deeper questions?* The word *amuse* combines two words, *a* and *muse.* It literally means "not" and "to ponder," or not to think. Why pursue experiences or amusements and not make evaluations? Because absolute values have been eliminated in society. And promoters understand the appetites of the American public so well that they can predict the anticipated economic returns for these amusements. Whether understood or not, economics has become the national standard. Cash is esteemed, and everything else is a nonissue.

As legal counsel for the Central Florida Citrus Bowl, Chris Kay is hired to lure the best possible New Year's bowl game to Orlando. Along with other representatives of the major bowls, Kay attends annual meetings to make presentations before the conference commissioners of the ACC, the Big East, the Big 10, the Big 8, the Southeast Conference, the Southwest Conference, and the Pac 10. Every representative brings extremely lucrative offers to bid for prime-time holiday games. Each portfolio includes multimillion-dollar television contracts normally sweetened by promises of additional millions coming from ticket sales or city tax revenues. While not the highest offer, Orlando's bid for the '95 New Year's bowl amounted to over $100 million over six years, including the sale of tickets.

When asked about all this fervor, Kay said, "Evidently the networks think these events can generate this kind of money from the advertisers." This decision, like so many others in sports, is made by asking the one question that drives the process—will it work economically in the cases of many cities trying to lure sports teams? No one considers the drain on city tax revenues that is used as bait and that could shore up decaying infrastructures. Experience is the highest good in society's cultural mind-set. Football is a necessity, and the public will pay any price to get it.

Fatalism is the third cultural mind-set. If people aren't in a position to make things happen, or they don't have the power to influence others, then they figure it's useless to try. Although they may stumble on a stimulating life experience accidentally, these people have never been stimulated from understanding the impact one person can have on another. This type of inspiration doesn't come from a ride at Walt Disney World; it springs from great ideas expressed in great books. On a number of occasions, I've watched people change through reading the printed page. Perhaps they begin to read the classics—both the secular and the religious. Like laying a new foundation brick by brick, each book lays a new thought and motivation. Eventually, they overcome the inertia in their lives, and things happen.

Although the fatalism of our culture has a strong gravitational pull, we can experience the joys of orbit in a new direction. And we can begin to escape one of many restrictions imposed from culture.

A Constant Bombardment of Information

"Flight 445 dove into a ravine. There were no survivors."

"Speaker of the House Newt Gingrich took a jab at the administration today. . . ."

Sound bites of information are constantly in our ears and mind. Reporters don't want the whole story. They want five-second sound bites for the top of the broadcast as a teaser. Politicians package economic plans and philosophical ideals to be heard and digested instantly. Their motto is "Give them what they can stand, not understand." The public is conditioned for these short bursts of information. If they are not brief, many people in the audience drift into boredom.

Because our news arrives in brief spurts, a lot of ground can be covered—and then repeated throughout the day. If the story is particularly traumatic, such as with the civil war in Bosnia or the horror stories of genocide in Rwanda, we become emotionally exhausted and quickly tire of it. Through the news, movies, and television, we have been trained to go through story lines and emotional gyrations in a half hour to two hours. But diligent study takes weeks and months.

What Does Diligent Study Mean?

In order for us to study diligently, we first need to determine what to study. Then, as we study, we can resolve critical issues, such as the issues of authority, knowledge, evil, and the supernatural.

Determine What to Study

The Puritans taught that, from God's perspective, everything in life was important. They approached life with intense practicality because theology applied to all areas of human experience. The minister studied botany, and the carpenter studied the Bible. With this guiding principle, they saw Bible study as foundational to all truth. Although the Bible doesn't give

99

scientific explanations, it reveals the source of scientific truth and explains how those truths fit in relation to God's overall scheme.

Diligent study is applauded *and* cautioned in the Bible. Warnings were issued from the two wisest men who walked this earth: Solomon and Jesus.

Solomon said, "Of making many books there is no end, and much study wearies the body" (Ecclesiastes 12:12). He refers to the vain pursuit of knowledge from dry wells and explains that the source of knowledge is the Lord of the universe. It is conceited for man to attempt to know anything about life without God.

Jesus gives a similar warning. Addressing the religious experts of his day, he said, "You diligently study the Scriptures because you think that by them you possess eternal life. These are the Scriptures that testify about me, yet you refuse to come to me to have life" (John 5:39-40). Some people pursue scriptural knowledge just for the sake of knowledge. The point is clear: Not all words that enter the eye engage the brain.

On the positive side, here are three encouraging results from the study of the Scriptures.

Bible study leads to success. Joshua 1:8 says, "Do not let this Book of the Law depart from your mouth; meditate on it day and night, so that you may be careful to do everything written in it. Then you will be prosperous and successful." The meditation (study) is linked to obedience and is part of the complete requirements for God's blessing.

Bible study invites God's participation. Ezra 7:9-10\states, "For the gracious hand of his God was on him. For Ezra had devoted himself to the study and observance of the Law of the Lord, and to teaching its decrees and laws in Israel."

Bible study marks a man as being serious about his craft. In 2 Timothy 2:15, Paul says, "Do your best [study] to present yourself to God as one approved, a workman who does not need to be ashamed and who correctly handles the word of truth."

Study Resolves Critical Issues

Whether people know it or not, four critical issues define their rationality—and in each of these areas, their opinion is already established. Culture may already have defined it for them. The first issue is *authority:* What tradition or laws govern our behavior? The second issue is *knowledge:* How is truth determined, and when does that information become an authority? The third is *evil:* What is its source, dominion, and role in our lives? Finally, the fourth issue is *the supernatural:* Do the laws of nature bind God in his operation? If not, how do we determine what constitutes a miracle?

The issue of authority. Whose glance do we feel peering over our shoulder? Which voice whispers in our ear? The list of options is large. Decisions aren't made without the influence of parents, children, peers, a sense of duty, and religious heritage. Choice cannot be made without conscious and subconscious influences.

At some point, we make a deliberate choice about the ultimate authority in our lives. If we don't consciously choose, then through happenstance we've still made a choice. We are not coerced by a malevolent authority, and we are not slaves; instead we need to consider what ultimately controls our lives.

Oswald Chambers said, "If I submit to the authority of a person it must be demonstrated that that person is greater than I am on the 'worthy' line. . . . If he is greater there, then I will bow down to his authority at once." Although Chambers refers to Christ, his point is universal. Our authority should not shackle us but free us. It should allow us to be more than we can be on our own and provide a sense of power for our undivided allegiance.

As the Word of God, the Bible is such an authority. Not an

archaic collection of Hebrew myths, the Bible is historically reliable. In two thousand years, not one archeological discovery has uncovered anything to dispute the text. From the Ebla tablets to the Dead Sea Scrolls, each discovery confirms the names, places, and events of Scripture.

Throughout sixty-six books, the messages are consistent and form a unified theme. Each points to a God who covenants with his people, who are sinful, like us. However, because of God's faithfulness, he creatively works through history on their behalf. God foretells about the Messiah, then he delivers on his promise. The sacrifice of God's Son provides salvation to everyone who accepts it.

The people who delivered this message came from diverse backgrounds. Moses was raised in the courts of Pharaoh; Joshua was a general. David was a king; Amos was a shepherd. In the New Testament, people like Matthew the tax collector, Luke the physician, and Peter the fisherman shared the gospel.

Other historical chronicles hide the weaknesses of their heroes—but not the Bible. The lead characters are introduced, warts and all. Most people know about David's affair with Bathsheba or Peter's denial of his Lord. Abraham faithfully followed God's call to an unfamiliar land and then, during a side trip to Egypt, lied about Sarah being his wife. Moses, the greatest leader of Israel, angrily struck the wilderness rock for water and was banned from entering the Promised Land. And yet, through all the pages of Scripture, there is never one mention of Jesus sinning while walking the earth. He was sinless.

Through the authority of the Bible, we are provided liberty. God's Word reveals stories of men and women lifted from defeat to victory. Through these stories we are motivated to overcome our circumstances. Also, the stories draw the curtain on a holy God, who embodies truth for powerful living here and forever in eternity.

When Christ came, the authority shifted from a document to God himself. Jesus Christ is the source of life. When the crowds heard Jesus speak, they said he spoke as "one who had authority" (Matthew 7:29). Although the intelligent religious minds tried to trap Jesus, they couldn't. He spoke truth and said he was the Truth. He lived a completely consistent life. He told people to love their enemies and then followed through on his words by eating with the "hated" tax collectors. He talked about the kingdom of God; then through his miracles, he demonstrated power from God's kingdom. His final earthly act wasn't a triumphant ride over his enemies. Instead, he allowed a humiliating execution. The committed Christian understands that no other authority is worthy of our obedience except God.

The issue of knowledge. Knowledge is more than adding layers of information into our mental computer. In a biblical sense, we pursue knowledge to gain wisdom. Have you met an extremely intelligent person who at the same time was unwise? These people can spout technical jargon or overwhelm you with scientific data, but they don't have the skills for social relationships.

King Solomon had knowledge but also balanced it with wisdom. He could ridicule the excessive pursuit of knowledge and then say, "But the advantage of knowledge is this: that wisdom preserves the life of its possessor" (Ecclesiastes 7:12). True wisdom preserves life. Wisdom allows us to deal with every aspect of our existence. For knowledge to preserve wisdom, it must exhibit at least four characteristics.

First, knowledge must be *unbiased* and *discerning*. Anyone with preconceived prejudice is searching only for propaganda, not knowledge. King Solomon called such people "mockers" and said they would never find wisdom (Proverbs 14:6). Cotton Mather's opponents were a good example of "mockers." These physicians scorned Mather's ideas because they assumed a minister couldn't know anything about combating a disease like smallpox.

People new to Christian faith always risk the danger of modern-day cults. Because these people are not discerning, they can join a cult without knowing it. A cult is a group that denies one or more of the major tenets of the parent religion—or it may add other sources of revelation. Knowledgeable people check out the doctrines of their faith and don't need a charismatic leader to interpret truth. A wise person always checks for a biased bent, especially from those who control the information.

Second, knowledge is also *comprehensive.* As committed Christians, we should be immersed in a constant flow of information. Our pursuit of truth never stops. We read everything about a given subject—including both positions. For a while I subscribed to *New Age Journal.* It raised a few eyebrows between the postman and the secretaries who sort my mail. But I decided to learn about the beliefs of the New Age movement. A few months ago, I canceled my subscription—not because the information shocked me. Instead I found the articles repetitive, biased, and uninteresting.

For a comprehensive view of knowledge, a person has to be disciplined. Solomon said, "Whoever loves discipline loves knowledge, but he who hates correction is stupid" (Proverbs 12:1). Solomon understood that wise people love a mental challenge. They feed on debate, and if proven wrong, they consider it gain, not humiliation. Cotton Mather never stopped studying nature. From his communications with friends, we learn that his scientific observations numbered over one hundred. In one letter, enclosed in a box of six or seven American plants, Mather gave the earliest known account of plant hybridization.

Third, knowledge needs to be *attested to by others over time.* Dozens of commentators have their own opinions about each difficult passage in Scripture. Varying treatises on subjects extend back to the early church fathers. "I've found a new and unique interpretation for this section of the Bible," someone will say. But that person would be wise to check that truth against the best minds from the past two thousand years. Like cream, truth rises and stays at the top. Certain subjects have great minds on both sides of the issue. A wise person understands that, in some areas, knowledge will always be incomplete.

Finally, *truth or knowledge must stand the test of time.* Truth cannot be contradicted. If it is contradicted, then everyone returns to the information. Was it biased and not comprehensive? In the case of the smallpox vaccinations, the colonial physicians refused to reconsider their underlying information until the remarkable recovery rate forced them to look again.

Our learning will impact us at different levels. "I believe Dave is a better athlete than John," says one person. That person holds a belief based on opinion. When new knowledge is introduced, that type of belief is quickly disregarded.

Some knowledge is culturally filtered. It is peripheral. We learn it from family or community, but we can abandon it without guilt once we realize there is a source of information larger than both.

When knowledge is gained from authorities, it is difficult to disregard, though it may not change our lives. Information is constantly fluctuating. Maybe we believe *I'm the captain of my own ship or the controller of my own fate* because college professors were so convincing. At first, everything goes fine. Then one day someone shares with us information that threatens that worldview. We learn about a sovereign God who is the master of our fate. Now we have to make a choice, and real convictions are etched into our being. We've wrestled with truth and discovered God's perspective.

The issue of evil. The first fifteen minutes of every evening news broadcast scream of evil—murder, robbery, or rape. In part, the national obsession with the O. J. Simpson trial was an attempt for us to understand how someone so liked allegedly committed such a hideous crime.

Philosophers and sociologists say evil comes from either human ignorance (as did Socrates and Plato) or imperfection. After all, "to err is human." As wonderful as it is, everything in creation has aberrations. Unfortunately, some err on a grander scale, like Hitler or Stalin. Though horrified by such potential for pervasive evil, we look good by comparison. But underneath we know we all are radically corrupt.

What is the solution? We are told that knowledge eventually frees mankind from evil. Did Hitler need more knowledge? Through knowledge, Hitler found more efficient ways to exterminate the "undesirables" from Germany. As he gained more information, Hitler dabbled in the occult, becoming more maniacal and incoherent in his demands. After pondering the issue of evil for a lifetime, Plato assumed the existence of an evil world-soul. Socrates admitted evil might be the work of a cosmic power.

The Bible paints a different picture. From a scriptural viewpoint, man is radically corrupt to the core. No part of his mind, heart, or psyche has escaped this corruption, though he may not fully unleash the fury of his evil. As the Desert Storm soldiers found out, nothing escaped the sand. The grit wouldn't go away. Sand was everywhere. The soldiers found it in their underwear, their eyes, tents, and guns. It about drove them crazy.

The same holds true for evil. While humans still perform marvelous feats and while science, technology, and medicine continue to expand exponentially, evil and crime rates accelerate in tandem. Why? The same person who is marvelously creative is also defiant. A person's moral behavior reveals his or her heart. God's commentary about his chosen people shows the extent of this stubbornness: "But they did not listen or pay attention; instead, they followed the stubborn inclinations of their evil hearts" (Jeremiah 7:24).

According to the psalmist, people act like decent human beings while at the same time harboring malice in their hearts (Psalm 28:3). Jesus agreed: "For from within, out of men's hearts, come evil thoughts, sexual immorality, theft, murder, adultery, greed, malice, deceit, lewdness, envy, slander, arrogance and folly" (Mark 7:21-22). The Bible leaves no misunderstanding about the source of evil.

Not only does evil come from the human heart, it leaves its victims spoiled and useless. Jesus said bad trees produce bad fruit and have to be discarded because they are useless. That's why so much emphasis is placed on the restoring power that comes from a relationship with Christ. People hate to feel dirty and gritty, but they also hate to feel worthless.

Evil is manifested in belligerence. A hardness and deadness of attitude infuriates God. That's why he used a verbal two-by-four to hit the Pharisees between the eyes. You don't call someone a "brood of vipers" unless that's the only language they understand. Of all people, these religious leaders should have understood the source and the dominion of evil. But they just wanted to maintain the power and the influence of their position.

The Bible says the prime mover behind evil is the evil one. Every beat of the heart and every inch of the earth is contested territory. King David not only was at war with his lust and deceitfulness, he had to contend with the enemy of all souls, Satan: "Satan rose up against Israel and incited David to take a census of Israel" (1 Chronicles 21:1). Jesus said the evil one delights in confusing potential believers or trying to prevent them from hearing news that would change their hearts. The struggle against the underworld forces of evil is an all-out war.

Distinguishing between a frontal assault from this evil one and the malice of our hearts is not easy. If we deny a personal representative of evil, we deny the words of Jesus and the larger scope of Scripture.

The issue of the supernatural. Miracles are the first things that come to mind when someone mentions the supernatural. Yet, there are different kinds of miracles. During a 1972 football playoff game, Terry Bradshaw, quarterback for the Pittsburgh Steelers, attempted to throw a pass to Frenchie Fuqua. Instead, it bounced off Jack Tatum of the Oakland Raiders. Steeler Franco Harris stood in the right spot at the right time. Harris scooped up the ball and ran it in for a touchdown, and Pittsburgh won the game. The sportscasters referred to it as the "immaculate reception," meaning that it was impressive. A person may see such a play only once or twice in a lifetime.

We can observe the majesty of cosmic events such as comet Shoemaker-Levy 9 punching holes in Jupiter. Scientists talk about this as a once-in-a-million-years event. We can appreciate the wonder and power of God, who created such an awesome universe.

A miracle also refers to remarkable timing. As R. C. Sproul points out, the star of Bethlehem perhaps had a natural or scientific cause, but it appeared at a very opportune time: "The extraordinary alignment of a group of stars, or a supernova may explain its brightness. To concede this possibility, however, makes the event no less a miracle."[2] Every human has witnessed an event with critical timing where deciding not to go or leaving five minutes earlier or making a phone call has made a tremendous difference. But this is not the kind of supernatural event where God overrules nature.

Jesus was involved with numerous miraculous occurrences. Some were obvious; others not so obvious. For instance, it's a miracle that the Son of God didn't perform more miracles. He could have. But sometimes Jesus perceived people were more interested in the performance than his overall message of being transformed by the new birth and entering a new kingdom. When that was the case, Christ refused to deliver another showstopper. It was miraculous that he allowed men to spit in his face, rip the flesh from his back, and crucify him. No other god of any other religion would subject himself to such ridicule. If the Christian story is not true, it is an embarrassing and ridiculous fabrication. Surely the inventors could have designed a god more in keeping with the gods of their day.

The obvious miracles revealed the power of God and also something about the nature of those who witnessed the miracles. The people who lost swine in the region of the Gerasenes learned something about the nature of demon possession: not only that a man could be released from such powers but also that demons needed bodies to inhabit, even pigs. We learn something about the swineherds, who preferred their economic conditions not be altered, even when a man's life was at stake: "Then the people began to plead with Jesus to leave their region" (Mark 5:17).

Jesus' miracles spotlight faith, but they are not always the prerequisite. The woman who touched Jesus' cloak was healed because of her faith (Mark 5:24ff.). Jesus refused to perform miracles in Nazareth because of the lack of faith (Matthew 13:53-58). At other times, the person healed had no clue what was going on or even believed the wrong thing. In John 9:1-5, as Jesus and his disciples walked along a road, they spotted a man blind from birth. The disciples asked a question that showed they were theologically off-base. They assumed the man's blindness was somebody's fault, that someone had sinned and this poor man was paying the consequences. Jesus didn't ask the man if he had faith; he healed him because he wanted to and so he could teach the disciples another important spiritual lesson.

The miracles of Jesus are called *signs* because they point to another promise or another event. These miracles weren't haphazard occasions to arouse the awe of the crowds but deliberate lessons about what we can expect in the future when Jesus actually reigns as king over the affairs of mankind. For instance, the casting out of the demons exhibits how Jesus has invaded the realm of Satan. Jesus' raising the dead points to the day when death will ultimately be defeated. His healing of the sick gives us hope for a day when suffering will cease. The miraculous feedings from Christ show that one day our physical needs will end. Those who witnessed the stilling of the storms could look forward to the time when there will be no more natural catastrophes.

God can and does intervene in the lives of people. We can't predict his intervention. We can't force his hand, tame him, or make him sit up on command. But if people experience a true occasion of the supernatural, they react as those in the Bible reacted—with astonishment and fear. David shouted, "You are awesome, O God" (Psalm 68:35). Those who observed Peter healing a crippled beggar were filled with "wonder and amazement" (Acts 3:10). But others were shaken to the core. When Jesus calmed the storm, the disciples were terrified and asked, "Who is this? Even the wind and the waves obey him!" (Mark 4:41).

To encounter an act of God is unnerving. Those who do so know they are on holy ground. The blood rushes from their face, their knees grow weak, and the word *miracle* is never again used in a flippant manner. They don't feel compelled to broadcast what happened, for it is a personal, intimate occasion like a shared secret between a husband and wife.

The Bottom Line
Your life of diligent study can begin anywhere and anytime. It starts with a commitment, then moves to finding a field of

110

study that interests you. You don't have to have a master's degree to master a subject. You just need the willingness to buy or borrow books and the interest in carving out daily time slots to crawl away with your books. For some, it may be an hour before work; for others, it may be the last hour of the day.

Jim Birchwood has the kind of job where he can read a few pages now and then while at work. Several times each day, I pass by his security guard station in the reception area of First Presbyterian Church. He greets me with a friendly smile as he puts his finger in a book to mark his place. He's always reading; sometimes he has stacks of books on a table in the hallway. Jim, now forty-nine, was a schoolteacher in the public schools for nine years. You could take the man out of the school but not the school out of the man.

One day my curiosity was aroused. "What and why are you reading, Jim?" I asked.

"I usually read mysteries, history, theology, and biblical studies," he responded. "If I'm not reading, I'm bored to tears. I've got to keep my mind active."

Active is an understatement. Jim reads fifty to seventy-five books a year. How different from the average adult, who, after he or she gets out of school, reads very few books. Half of the people who go to college never read another book after they graduate. Jim is currently studying for the deaconate of the Episcopal Church and is in charge of adult education at his local parish church.

I asked Jim about the perceived benefits of his study program. "A lot of people try to read the Bible in a vacuum. They don't understand the history. They also don't understand the impact of the Jewish culture, traditions, and history on the people in the days when Jesus was on earth." That's why Jim does a lot of digging in the works of Josephus.

Jim probably doesn't realize the influence he has on people who pass by his desk every day. He's doing everything that can be asked of a person who wants to take his Christianity seriously. With established goals for his continuing education, Jim takes courses and seminars whenever his schedule will allow. At every opportunity, Jim cracks open a book. The motto for First Presbyterian Church, established by its senior minister, J. Howard Edington, has been "a teaching church." Little did he know that motto would stretch from the security guard to the pastor.

Finally, nothing makes you want to study more than to be called on to teach. If you are serious about being diligent in study, then offer to teach. You may surprise yourself; you may even find an avocation. No one ever learns more than the teacher. If you don't have the skills to get up in front of large crowds, then start a small discussion group. When people want to know what you have to say, not how you say it, then you'll know how wisely you have invested your time. Diligent study is another sign of a committed Christian.

THINKING IT THROUGH

1. In what ways do you think culture has influenced your mind-set? Be as specific as possible.

2. When do you feel you are hearing propaganda rather than receiving new knowledge?

3. What do the following verses have to say about study?

   - Joshua 1:8
   - Ezra 7:10
   - Proverbs 14:6
   - John 5:39-40
   - Acts 17:16-34
   - 2 Timothy 2:15

4. Do you feel diligent study can ever be a problem? If so, when? If not, why not?

5. What prevents you from spending more time studying? List one book you could read in the next month to help you begin good study habits.

6. Do you believe God still performs supernatural acts? If so, give an example. If not, why not?

6

Mentor Others

*"Truly intelligent people know they have not been
self-educated. . . . The truly educated have been mentored,
either in person or by reading or association, by superior
minds with greater skills and mature spirits."*

FRED SMITH

A LIFELONG desire for Dr. John Tolson was to be a coach. In
college, Tolson started out to study coaching. Instead, he became a minister and founded a ministry of evangelism and
discipleship for men called The Gathering.

But the idea of coaching continued to dog him. Tolson's
love for basketball nearly matched his obsession to teach the
Bible. In Houston, he began the basketball chapel program for

the NBA Rockets. Then when he moved to Orlando, Tolson played matchmaker with Pat Williams and businessman Jimmy Hewitt. It produced the Orlando Magic. Tolson's free throw–shooting ability is a legend. He's been known to go to Magic practices and wager his skills against any of the NBA's finest. If they take him on, these players usually lose. It's difficult to beat a 95 percent average.

One summer Tolson's teaching ministry slowed down proportionately with the rising Florida heat and humidity. Itching for a new challenge, Tolson and two friends, David Todd from Texas and Orlando attorney Chris Kay, started to dream about a weeklong basketball camp for inner-city kids ages eight through thirteen. Before long they raised the money to rent a couple of gymnasiums, hire some coaches, print T-shirts, and buy basketballs and trophies. The camp was off and running. Instead of one week, they had enough kids for the camp to extend to three weeks. On the opening day of camp, a Disney band, including Mickey and Goofy, welcomed the kids when they got off the bus. It was showtime. Coach Tolson was in his element.

On the final day of camp, in a stirring challenge to the men from The Gathering, Tolson asked, "Are you willing to mentor between one and three of these boys for a year after the camp is over?" The men looked around at each other. What a challenge! Most were middle-aged white men with little in common with inner-city African American boys. Mentoring may not have been the right word . . . it was more like corralling. The men were given some basic instructions about activities with the boys and how to start building a relationship. Tolson left the rest of the program to the creativity of each person.

One of them was Dr. Frank Tew, a cardiologist, who grew up in North Carolina. Tew had always felt that young African Americans were given a raw deal from society. Despite a thriving practice in Orlando, Tew took advantage of every occasion to study about the plight and rage of African Americans. He had an insatiable appetite to grow.

When I sponsored a weeklong missions trip to the Dominican Republic to build a small school in a poor barrio outside Santo Domingo, Tew went with us. Since we roomed together, we would talk late into the night. He would ask me what books I thought were worth reading and then would make careful notes. Tew wanted his life to count.

When Tolson asked for volunteers for the First Step Basketball program, Tew was one of the first to sign up. "I really didn't know what to do," Tew later admitted. "I felt awkward. I'm not an African American role model or a famous athlete to attract these kids' attention. I just wanted to establish some kind of bond."

Tew was assigned a thirteen-year-old named John Jackson. During their first meeting, they ate hamburgers together at a local restaurant. If Tew was going to be visiting Jackson's neighborhood, he knew the first step would be to get to know Jackson's mother. As this middle-aged white man drove past the hangout where men congregated at the corner store to deal cards (or more valuable substances), the neighborhood needed an explanation. Later Tew learned that Jackson used a password—"Frank's all right; he's my *mentor.*" The word *mentor* was synonymous with respect.

What Tew hadn't bargained for was Jackson's brothers, sisters, and cousins who also wanted in on this new friendship. Eager to establish these relationships, Tew obliged up to the number of people who could fit into his car. Tew and his wife, Monica, took them to Magic games, Universal Studios for Halloween night, and the circus. One night Tew was so excited about taking four kids to the circus that he jumped out of the car in the parking lot and left it running . . . the whole time he was inside the arena. Two hundred dollars later—after each kid had consumed two small pizza supremes, cotton candy, and Tew had bought a few souvenirs as mementos—the group returned to his car. Tew found this note: "Thank you for the nice car, and thank you for keeping it running for me." Fortunately, the kind person had turned the car off and left Tew's keys in the ignition.

Later, Tew gave money to Jackson's mother, Shirley, and stepfather, Charlie, to take the family to Walt Disney World. Sadly, Charlie died from a brain tumor not long afterward. The loss of his stepfather was hard for Jackson. Even with a mentor helping wherever he could, Jackson slipped in and out of trouble. Now every kid in the Jackson family is a concern to Frank and Monica Tew. But among the Jackson clan, the Tews have earned the right to encourage and to confront.

"Frank, don't you get discouraged sometimes and wonder if it is worth it all?" I asked.

He didn't hesitate with his answer. "Some aren't going to make it . . . the statistics are against them. But that doesn't mean each one has to become a statistic. Maybe we can make a difference with one or two. When you get to know them, you see their great personalities and wonderful potential."

No matter what happens, Frank and Monica Tew won't give up. After Charlie's death, Shirley nearly had enough money from the insurance settlement for a down payment on a small, one-thousand-square-foot home. Tew provided the balance of the down payment. His wife's brother-in-law brokered the sale, then gave his commission check to the family as a housewarming gift. Monica Tew is teaching Jackson's mother, Shirley, to balance her checkbook. Every chance he gets, Frank Tew checks in on the kids. The word *mentor* has a good reputation in that neighborhood.

There are two types of mentors—those who try the big brother approach with younger kids like the First Step Basketball program. Then there is the more classical relationship between a mentor and his apprentice. *Webster's* defines mentoring as "a trusted counselor or guide." Bobb Biehl, who has written widely about mentoring, says it's "more like having a loving uncle. This uncle cares if you live or die and salutes your success." The remainder of this chapter deals primarily with the second approach, although many of the principles transfer to the big brother option.

Mentoring: Something Old . . . Something New?

Although *mentoring* may be a relatively new term, the concept of mentoring has been around since early days—through the work of craftsmen, the example of Scripture, and the roles of family members.

Vocational Role Models

Throughout history, apprenticeship was a type of mentoring. Carpenters, composers, and masons learned their trade at the side of the masters. They also learned about perseverance until they excelled in their craft—and about what it meant to be honest with themselves and their customers.

At age thirteen Michelangelo was assigned as an apprentice to the painter Ghirlandajo. From the master, Michelangelo learned techniques that one day he would use in painting the ceiling of the Sistine Chapel in the Vatican. This kind of master/apprentice relationship is documented all the way back to the laws of Hammurabi of Babylon, in the eighteenth century B.C. It was a way of ensuring that enough craftsmen would always be available. During medieval times, it was common for the apprentice to sleep in the shop of the master craftsman. Sometimes the apprentice married the master's daughter. Unfortunately, the Industrial Revolution and mass production dealt a deathblow to the personal relationship side of apprenticeship when job training replaced the mentoring process.

Individual training survived beyond the Middle Ages, primarily through the university system and the master's degree. But these classrooms were one of the few places where personal attention was given to equip young and talented protégés over an extended period of time.

Biblical Role Models of Mentoring

From a Christian perspective, mentoring doesn't simply sharpen talent; it develops character with a lasting impact on this world for the kingdom of God. Although you won't find the term *mentoring* in the Bible, the concept can be seen in the lives of people from Genesis to Revelation. A young Joshua learned how to follow God faithfully at the feet of Moses; Ruth wanted to be adopted by the people of Naomi after she had observed how God helped Naomi handle the tragedies of life; the commander Abishai was willing and eager to kill those who opposed David but learned principles of honor and submission through heeding his master's wisdom; Barnabas poured his life into John Mark. When Paul thought John Mark was a washed-up traitor, Barnabas vigorously defended his protégé. Each protégé, in turn, went on to make a difference. Mentors are looking for that sort of payoff.

Family Role Models of Mentoring

In a recent small group meeting, one of the discussion questions was, "What is the most important thing in your life?" My first thought was to say "Jesus." It wouldn't have been a lie, but it seemed obvious. Then I considered my rapidly approaching fiftieth birthday and my new grandson, Ian. A dozen thoughts skipped across my mind about what I would one day like to share with him. So I said, "I want to leave a legacy for my family and friends."

Sadly, when you examine the statistics about the family in America, our family is in the minority. Today my daughter, Erica, is returning home after graduating from college. She will be living with us until either graduate school or a job takes her away again. My son, Brett, his wife, Heather, and their son, Ian, live in our area of Orlando, no more than twenty minutes away. Heather's parents live thirty minutes in the other direction. Aunts and uncles from both families live within the same range. Most attend the same church.

Ian's situation is an abnormality in America. Because our society is so mobile, most kids are lucky to have one other member of a nuclear family within shouting distance. Mentoring specialist Bobb Biehl says that 60 percent of the population lives over five hundred miles from aunts and uncles and grandparents. Who is there besides the parent(s) to hug them, love them, and ask how they're doing? When parents have to make tough decisions and discipline their children, who can step in and support them? The rest of society could care less. Besides the parents, who would be saddened by the actions of a rebellious child? Who provides a sense of belonging and a sense of identity? Who affirms giftedness and gives children permission to be themselves?

That's why mentoring is so important. It satisfies the longings of both protégé and mentor. Some people don't even know they have holes in their hearts that mentoring can plug. Adults who live in faraway places, isolated from aging aunts, uncles, parents, and grandparents, need a coach. Information, which can come from instructors or those with the desire to disciple, may or may not be their particular need. These protégés need someone who can show them from their own personal experience. Then that mentor can cheer them on as they try out their new skills. They need an honest coach who won't lie or slap them on the back with gratuitous compliments.

Fred Smith, a retired businessman from Dallas, has written much on the subject of leadership and mentoring. Fred had the ambition to sing at the Metropolitan Opera. One day an older friend told him, "Fred, you have everything except talent, and without that, all the practice and discipline and hope will not accomplish what you want to be—so I suggest you find another field." Although the words were painful for Fred to hear, he listened and changed his life direction into business instead of music. There Fred blossomed—all because a coach was honest and willing to hurt him, yet cheer for him.

Why Mentor?

Most people desire to have someone besides their parents care for them. That's one reason church youth work or parachurch youth organizations have played such a vital role in the development of the next generation. Many youth workers are not much older than those they lead, but they become role models who understand their group's situation. They care deeply about these junior or senior high school students.

Young adults also face upheaval as they begin new careers or possibly try to raise a family. If they pause long enough to lift their masks, they will admit their fears. These young people may have plenty of friends, and they aren't looking for heroes. Instead, they need someone with compassion, understanding, and a lot of wisdom.

So first, *young people are searching for a mentor with mileage.* Actually, they may require several mentors. Perhaps one person can provide guidance in professional life, another in spiritual life. Sometimes one person is a "two-for-one special." Age has little to do with who is the mentor. It has more to do with respect.

A second reason for mentoring is *to leave a legacy that extends beyond the circle of influence.* One of the little-known names connected to mentoring is Sherwood Anderson. One day a man moved to Chicago so he could be near Anderson. For the next year, the two men were inseparable, whether taking walks or eating together. The younger man wrote stories, and Anderson critiqued his work. At the completion of their time together, this young man went off and wrote *The Sun Also Rises.* That young man was Ernest Hemingway. After Hemingway moved away, Anderson, in search of a new venue, moved to New Orleans. He met a poet who was writing a novel. Mentor and protégé worked through every page. The novel was published as *Soldier's Pay.* The protégé was William Faulkner. Also while in New Orleans, Anderson taught writers like Thomas Wolfe and playwright William Saroyan. After several years, Anderson moved to California, where he spent nine months with another budding writer—John Steinbeck.

Literary historian Malcolm Cowley said, "No other American author has ever had such an impact on the next generation of writers as Sherwood Anderson." Anderson was devoted to mentoring young writers. Why? Probably because at the turn of the century, as a young man Anderson was part of the prestigious Chicago circle writing group, along with Theodore Dreiser and Carl Sandburg. Anderson knew about mentoring. He experienced it firsthand, then turned and mentored others. As Anderson said, "I help others write because it helped me write."

Qualifications for a Mentor

Several years ago, Ralph Veerman and I decided to concentrate on training people with an unusual talent and desire to impact the social, business, and professional structures of their city. We called the program the Greater Orlando Leadership Foundation (G.O.L.F., an appropriate acronym for Orlando). Our idea was to begin a one-day-a-month curriculum taught by some of our nation's finest communicators, such as R. C. Sproul, Os Guinness, and Senator Bill Armstrong. We felt that a mentoring relationship with another Christian businessperson or professional was a necessary component after completion of the program.

Guess what? We couldn't find people to be mentors. Why?

Because they didn't feel worthy. We should have made it clear we weren't looking for perfect mentors but for committed people who wanted to build their life into another person. Unfortunately, most of the people we invited declined because they had never been mentored themselves and therefore didn't feel qualified.

Who does qualify? When you look in the mirror, answer the following ten questions to see if you fit.

#1: Do You Love Christ?

If Christ asked you this question, how would you respond? From Scripture, it is apparent that those closest to Jesus were crazy about him. As author Brennan Manning says, "These biblical characters, however clean or tawdry their personal histories may have been, are not paralyzed by the past in their present response to Jesus. Tossing aside all self-consciousness they ran, clung, jumped and raced to Him."

If we love Christ, we'll want to invest in others just as Peter was told—"Feed my sheep." We'll forget the past and abandon excuses about "the time you did . . ." and "I'm unworthy because . . ." Also we'll realize that few Christians fully understand why or how we love Jesus. Most people respond to the emotional trappings of Christianity rather than to the man himself. They are stirred by music, motivated by orators, or maybe captivated by biblical stories. A mentor can help them forget about the props and get to know the chief Actor, Jesus Christ.

#2: Do You Genuinely Care about Someone?

Mentoring starts with a keen interest in the welfare of another person. This person may not know you care, but you watch him or her, inquire regularly, and observe carefully the person's progress. When you are together, conversation is effortless and you don't consider any time as wasted. This protégé is too young to be your peer or the kind of friend you would socialize with. In some ways, you would like to duplicate yourself through that person.

#3: Are You Committed to Growing Yourself?

This is critical. Many young adults suspect that older adults live boring lives. If you aren't constantly sharpening your mental and spiritual skills, it won't take long for protégés to smell staleness. However, they can be challenged from your enthusiasm for truth and willingness to dig for gold wherever it may be found. Mentoring can take place over many years. Unless you are connected to your own pipeline of mental nourishment, you can exhaust your wisdom in a short amount of time.

#4: Are You Willing to Be Vulnerable?

If you spend your time bragging about your accomplishments and attempt to make every conversation a teachable moment, soon you'll be talking to yourself. Nothing worthwhile in life is obtained without a struggle. One of the greatest lessons you can leave is how to persevere through adversity. To teach about adversity means admitting your times of weakness. How have you overcome the jaws of fear or at times dealt with the demons of self-doubt? It's hard to fake it since the feelings are written all over us when we're anxious. Admitting your weakness will take the pressure off your protégé to imitate a saint.

#5: Are You Willing to Affirm and Confront?

Both affirming and confronting are necessary in the mentoring process. Affirmation is not false compliments but genuine encouragement on a regular basis about some aspect of legitimate accomplishment. Loving confrontation is necessary for you to be taken seriously. Any protégés *want* to know about their strengths, but they *need* to know if they are heading down a path where they have little skill. The confrontation can be temporarily painful, but in the long run, your protégés will be eternally grateful for your candor because they can redirect themselves into an area where they have greater skills.

#6: Are You Willing to Walk the Talk?

This isn't a call for perfection but an honest attempt to practice what you preach. I am still in full-time Christian work today because a long list of models and a few mentors from Youth for Christ were genuine. They loved kids, prayed for them, and worked hard to give them opportunities to come to Christ. And they refused to manipulate kids for the sake of looking good or raising more money. No matter what profession you are in, your protégés need to see you battling the daily temptations unique to your calling. They won't expect you to bat 100 percent. But they want to follow those who struggle toward consistency when many others have given up.

#7: Are You Willing to Pray?

While it's not necessary to spend a lot of time praying with your protégé, it is important to talk to the Lord continually about him or her. The major battles of life are spiritual in nature, not earthly. As Charles Spurgeon, noted British minister of the nineteenth century, said, "Since the first hour in which goodness came into conflict with evil, it has never ceased to be true in spiritual experience, that Satan hinders us. From all points of the compass, all along the line of battle, in the vanguard and in the rear, at the dawn of day and in the midnight hour, Satan hinders us."

Protégés may be dealing with insecurities, anxieties, or even leftover childhood baggage that creates a monumental hindrance. There may be health issues or roadblocks to career advancement. Pray for your protégés as if their lives depended on it. They do.

#8: Are You Willing to Be Emotionally Independent?

Are you trying to fill an emotional hole in your life? If so, then don't try to fill that need through being a mentor. A certain emotional detachment is necessary so the mentor's peace of mind is not ratcheted to the accomplishments or failures of his protégé. It's impossible not to get involved emotionally, but if the ego is invested, that attachment can become an illness. One's own sense of worth can be threatened by the failures of another person.

#9: Are You Willing to Spend Time?

It's difficult to make an impact on another person's life without spending a lot of time. During the first phase of a relationship, people are posturing, trying to make an impression on each other. It takes time to discover how each person will respond to off-the-wall comments, as well as deeply held convictions. Protégés will want to know if they are safe to express their thoughts freely (even if those thoughts might be offensive). Also they want to know how you handle non-productive or even ill-defined thoughts. The goal between a mentor and protégé is to create a climate where thinking can be done out loud—without a defined agenda. Actually such conversation may be more fruitful than it seems. Part of the joy of mentoring comes from mutual discovery after a relaxed period of verbal bantering.

#10: Do You Want to See a Protégé Succeed?

It's impossible to care for protégés or to work for their success if you are competing with them or potentially jealous of their accomplishments. But if you see your sense of purpose enhanced from another's good fortune, then you are a prime candidate to become a mentor.

What's the Difference between Mentoring and Discipling?

Some people believe mentoring is too difficult, and it would be easier to just focus on discipling, which doesn't carry the risks that come with a long-term mentoring commitment.

However, discipleship is primarily content-oriented. Some people may feel *unqualified* to be a mentor because of past failures, but more people feel *disqualified* because they believe their intellect is inadequate.

One July in Boulder, Colorado, at the Promise Keepers Leadership Conference, Bobb Biehl asked his audience, "How many feel comfortable doing evangelism?" Five percent responded. "How many feel comfortable discipling another person?" Another 15 percent responded. Then Bobb defined mentoring and asked the audience to respond depending on their comfort level. Seventy-five percent said they could see themselves in that role. Bobb explained the difference between evangelism, discipleship, and mentoring with the following chart.[1]

Function	Attitude	Whose Agenda?	Training	Time Frame
Evangelism	Respect	The evangelist	Requires evangelism training	One hour
Discipleship	Respect	Based on content	Takes intellectual maturity	Limited
Mentoring	Personal chemistry	The protégé	Practical life experience	Long-term

Bobb Biehl suggests that we think carefully about the following three questions before we jump into a mentoring role with anyone:

1. Are you ego-centered? Do you honestly have the present frame of mind to think about anyone besides yourself? Maybe because of your job, health, or family, you are in the middle of a difficult personal experience. You find yourself self-consumed, not by choice, but by circumstances beyond your control. Now may not be the time to be a mentor.

2. Are you a driven person? Driven people care more for accomplishments than relationships. A protégé is not a task to be scratched off a to-do list. If people feel like a project, they feel used and manipulated—as if their mentor is using them to look good in accomplishing one more goal. Such personalities are better suited for street evangelism than mentoring.

3. Are you a young parent or the primary caregiver for other family members or friends? Your plate may be full, and you may not need another time-consuming relationship. Instead of investing in a protégé, put your efforts toward the one God has assigned to you at this time in life.

I Want to Be a Mentor: So What Do I Do Now?
Many books about mentoring are written to encourage a person to seek a mentor. They discuss the advantages and benefits of having this kind of relationship. Sadly for many, it's like getting all dressed up with no place to go. People desperately want a mentor but can't locate one.

This chapter deals with the flip side, sounding a trumpet call for mentors to search out protégés. Then these protégés can be launched into another stratum of effectiveness with loving guidance from someone who cares.

Whom Should I Pursue as a Protégé?
If you're ready to pursue a protégé, what qualities should you look for?

Someone whose chemistry connects with yours. It's a match if you look forward to being with this person. Your tastes are similar, and you laugh at the same kind of jokes. The same issues burden you, and your passions are similar. Without this chemistry, the prospect for a long-term relationship is dim.

Someone who shares your philosophy of life. This person needs to have the same Christian commitment and to be singing off the same theological page. Maybe this person doesn't have well-defined views on biblical issues, but he or she is hungry to learn and willing to hear your perspective.

Someone you want to see succeed. In mentoring, a sense of fulfillment is dependent on watching the protégé move ahead in family, career, and social arenas. If he or she exceeds your expectations and accomplishments, you are thrilled—not jealous.

Someone with patience and discipline. Most of us have heard the quip, "Success is one percent inspiration and 99 percent perspiration." To learn a craft is a lifelong process. Anything lifelong takes more commitment than many people can muster. This lack of commitment stems back to the culture. Patience and discipline are not virtues touted by the media. To locate someone with these traits is rare. But one day patient, disciplined people *will* make a difference—so seek them out!

Someone who is vulnerable. Unfortunately, vulnerability is often equated with weakness. On the positive side, it means not being defensive. Defensive people will make excuses for their mistakes and weaknesses; vulnerable people admit they need help and are willing to listen. Defensive people play games to mask their fears; vulnerable people deal realistically with pain as they go through the experience. The bottom line is, defensive protégés won't learn anything. They need a counselor more than a mentor.

Someone who doesn't idolize you. Every mentor wants to be liked and respected. But if the mentor needs to be worshiped, then an unwholesome dependence has been created. A quick means to resolve this problem is for the mentor to burst the protégé's bubble. The mentor must be vulnerable and share his or her own weaknesses, fears, and doubts. If the mentor is honest and the protégé continues to insist on acting like a subject before royalty, progress will be limited. Half of the joy of mentoring is discussion, which at times can be slightly heated.

Kent, a young man I have the joy of mentoring, doesn't take every mental morsel I deliver as a sacred offering. Often Kent disagrees; more often than not, he has a better thought. Fortunately, in the process he's very kind, and secretly I take great delight in his cogent arguments. Never for an instant do I feel as if I am the only source of guidance for his career or his spirituality. This lack of hyperreverence allows us to glean what we can from our relationship, then not worry about the rest.

Your protégé could be a nephew, a niece, or even a grandchild, but not a son or daughter. I don't include children because the roles of parent and mentor aren't the same. The parent's responsibility isn't dependent on personal chemistry or feelings of affection. It is an authority arrangement that involves love, teaching, and discipline and, I hope, is immersed in affection. In God's design, parents aren't given the option to affirm, pray, spend time with, or genuinely care for the child. Even if parents score high in all of these areas, the children are going to need someone else to believe in them. Children know their parents are supposed to be supportive, but they want to know if others will help because they see potential in them.

What Plan Should We Choose?

If you have located a person whom you would like to mentor, the first step is to take that person to lunch, if he or she agrees. (I also strongly recommend that men always mentor men, and women always mentor women. Between members of the opposite sex, emotional attachment sometimes leads to passionate exchanges.)

Begin the conversation explaining why you have selected this person as a protégé (unless that person has chosen you!). Then express your concern for his or her future welfare. At best, you have started a mentoring process. At worst, you have flattered someone you care about and given him or her a free lunch. Discuss what's involved in mentoring (in generalities). Then decide whether you want the relationship to be structured or casual.

A structured approach. Structure has a starting point, a framework, and an ultimate design. You and the protégé set a regular time to meet each month and go over an agenda. Probably both the mentor and the protégé should keep a notebook to measure progress. Bobb Biehl suggests that the agenda cover four points: decisions, problems, progress, and prayer. The decisions and problems can involve any aspect of life—family, financial, physical, professional, social, or spiritual. Then a plan is discussed and agreed on. From week to week, the progress is monitored, and midcourse corrections are made as necessary. Every meeting is closed in intercessory prayer for each other.

There's one major risk with the structured plan. Once you start, how do you stop? What if the relationship turns out to be disappointing and it drifts apart? Someone is going to feel bad. The protégé might get the idea that he or she really wasn't worthy of your mentoring. One way to protect yourself from this situation is to establish preset times for evaluation. During this evaluation period, each person discusses whether he or she wants to continue in the process. At some point, it may be best to shift from a structured strategy to a more casual approach.

A casual approach. In this method, the mentor deliberately establishes a relationship with the protégé. He wants this person to know that he cares about tracking his career, wants to be there for him, to get together as often as possible, and to do everything he can to see that person networked into successful social and professional structures. Also, the mentor commits to pray for and with his protégé on a regular basis.

These casual meetings have no formal agenda outside two genuine questions: How are you doing? How can I help? The two questions cover all areas of life. Sometimes they can be asked over the phone, other times over lunch or on the golf course. Sincerity is critical. After meeting together for a couple of months, the protégé will know whether you are simply playing a game or if you really care. A number of men have introduced me to others as one of their mentors. They considered me as more than a good friend. Although I didn't follow up with them on a regular basis, I did check up when I could. Sometimes I asked others for a favor on their behalf. It's amazing how little attention it took for me to be considered their mentor. Just think what could have happened if someone had really taken them under his wing!

How Can I Help My Protégé?

A good mentor is always thinking about how to help his or her protégé. This chapter began with the story of Dr. Frank Tew, who mentored an inner-city boy from the First Step Basketball Camp. One of the other mentors from this program, Ralph Veerman, travels each week around the United States because of the high demands for his consulting business. However, he still makes the time to check on his First Step kid. Ralph creates ways to motivate and help him for the long haul. One day Ralph went to a local bank and established a small but growing fund. Now this protégé will be able to attend college when he is old enough. When Ralph and his protégé began their mentoring program, the kid had no idea of the good that could come from his mentor's plans. He also didn't know how committed some people can be in following their Lord and loving fellow humans.

You can help your protégé in many ways. Plan a special outing, like a dinner or weekend retreat, for the older protégé. Provide a "scholarship fund" so husband and wife can get away together. What a boost to their marriage! Learn about special relatives and friends who are important to your protégé, then think creatively how to involve them in meaningful, encouraging ways.

Order special magazines or buy books that are timely for your protégé's progress. Work together on special service projects, such as serving a meal at a Christian center for the homeless or building a home for Habitat for Humanity. Always search for ways to help your protégé grow and stretch for higher goals.

These special occasions can't happen every week. No one could afford it—besides, you'd wear each other out! Timing is everything. But a good mentor is sensitive to fluctuating events. Know when to act and when to back off. Sometimes just be the loving aunt or uncle who is there—without an agenda or questions. And remember to pray—always. One day your protégé will find someone to mentor, and the mentoring cycle will continue.

The Bottom Line

Committed Christians build the mentoring process into their lives with people of all ages. They can't help but look for ways to spiritually challenge their closest friends—not in a patronizing way but "as iron sharpens iron, so one man sharpens another" (Proverbs 27:17). This includes sharpening the personality or character of another person, as well as sharpening each other's wits. Nothing will keep you more fresh, more challenged to grow than constantly thinking and discovering new things that benefit you and everyone around you.

Many times my fax machine whirs with an article or some other interesting tidbit from one of my mentoring brothers. In the strictest sense, we have no official mentoring relationship. But a mentor is someone who shows another how to navigate the maze. It takes time and effort for mentors to say to themselves, *Larry might be interested in this article,* and then to cut it out and fax it. They have to know me and what I'm dealing with in my life, and they have to be aware of the kind of information that would shed light on the path I travel.

In the final analysis, committed Christians deliberately seek to sharpen others: kids struggling on the wrong side of the tracks; young, emerging protégés who need the guidance of a veteran; friends who can be far more effective because of stimulating interaction. Christ's followers determine to make a difference, to target the ones they can best impact, and then let their arrows of mentoring fly.

THINKING IT THROUGH

1. What's the difference between mentoring and being a good friend?

2. Who mentored the following Bible characters?

   Joshua_____
   Ruth _____
   Abishai _____
   John Mark_____
   Timothy_____

3. If you were being mentored, would you prefer the structured approach or the casual approach? Why? If you were the one mentoring someone else, which approach would you prefer? Why?

4. Has anyone ever mentored you? If so, describe what he or she did. What was helpful to you? What was not?

5. Have you ever mentored someone? If so, what did you do? If not, what is your biggest obstacle in becoming a mentor?

6. Evaluate yourself. Are you ready to become a mentor? Why or why not? If you are, ask God to reveal to you someone you could mentor in the months ahead.

7

Live with a Passion

The people in our world who rise to the top of business, sports, academia, science, and politics usually do it because they are fueled by passion.   GORDON MACDONALD

JONATHAN Shirley nearly died during his senior year at the University of West Virginia. One cold and snowy afternoon, Jonathan and his roommate were hitchhiking back to school. A kind old man in a truck pulled over, and the two climbed inside. The three of them squeezed together with Jonathan's over-six-foot frame wedged into the middle.

They hadn't traveled more than a fraction of a mile when Jonathan felt a funny sensation in his chest. Suddenly he gasped and fell over on the driver. Jonathan was unconscious from a heart attack. Fortunately an Exxon station was immediately ahead. They pulled Jonathan out of the truck and laid him on the icy asphalt near the gas pumps.

His roommate tried mouth-to-mouth resuscitation, then the gas attendant tried to duplicate the CPR he had seen on TV emergency shows. Finally, the paramedics arrived on the scene. Jonathan not only survived the ordeal, but he gained a new perspective—that each day is a gift.

Although he's naturally inquisitive, now Jonathan is even more passionate about learning. After receiving an undergraduate degree in psychology, he earned a master's in forensics from George Washington University. Later Jonathan practiced tax law in Orlando—in between pursuing another degree in economics from the University of Central Florida plus studying theology many hours each week in preparation for teaching his Sunday school class.

If there's such a thing as a Renaissance man, Jonathan fits the ticket. He pursues with a vengeance whatever he tackles— whether piano, golf, or global economic theory. One day I asked Jonathan, "Why are you so interested in so many different areas?"

He responded, "I'm naturally and intellectually curious. For example, not long ago I prepared for a Sunday school lesson on 2 Samuel 2, which deals with the anointing of David as king of Judah. I didn't have the foggiest idea what anointing was all about. So I went to the bookstore and purchased some books that could shed some light on that subject. Although it was only a minor point in my overall lesson, I needed to know why David was so adamant about not touching God's anointed." Jonathan has a passion for learning.

Why is passion characteristic of a committed Christian? From the negative perspective, I've known many pew warmers whose only claim to spiritual fame was breathing air and taking up space. From a positive perspective, people like

Jonathan Shirley are passionate about their faith. Being around them is infectious!

Most dictionaries define *passion* as "depth of feeling toward anything that is accompanied by fervor, enthusiasm, and zeal." Passion is the fuel that makes the engine run; nothing goes without it. Passion gives life an extraordinary quality; it moves people beyond ordinary activities and accomplishments. For example, great novels, movies, works of art, military campaigns, and business triumphs are produced by passionate people.

There is also a negative side to passion: It can be destructive, irrational, and reactive. Any policeperson will tell you that most murders are crimes of passion. A jilted lover or jealous spouse explodes with fervor and feeling that is out of control. At best, unbridled passion is sad, and, at worst, it is frightening.

When unregulated passion overheats a person's system to the boiling point, it can't be indefinitely sustained. Sometimes a rally call, such as "Seize the moment" or "Strike while the iron is hot," will drive passionate people wild. However, while these slogans are motivating, they can't be continually followed without taking a break. Those who never reduce the heat are in danger of a meltdown.

Entering the Realms of Passion

There are four areas of life about which the committed Christian, in particular, is passionate: spiritual devotion, service to others, work and career, and everyday life.

Passionate in Spiritual Devotion

When Jesus was asked about the greatest commandment of the law, he replied, "Love the Lord your God with all your heart and with all your soul and with all your mind" (Matthew 22:37).

Passion for Christ should fill our every fiber. Christ wants us to feel that love, to reach the full capacity of our spiritual potential, to exercise our mind over great theological truths.

When a person enters a clinic or hospital for a checkup, the nurses first check the person's vital signs. Why? Because these signs are indicators of physical health. It's important to check our spiritual vital signs as well. If we have no burning desire to pursue God, then it's probably difficult to find the time or interest to read or to engage in thoughts that stretch our spiritual mental capacities.

The New Testament is a case study about the impact spiritually impassioned people have on the world. Paul's passion made him impervious to pain and fatigue in much the same way that NFL running backs are so focused on the goal line, so intent on gaining more ground, that they don't give a second thought to the pain of bone-crunching tackles. But Paul chased a goal far more worthy than six points on a scoreboard. He withstood hunger, beatings, shipwreck, and a debilitating thorn in the flesh to spread the gospel over the known world of the first century A.D. Paul embodied the greatest commandment from Jesus.

Passionate in Service to Others

Passionate people engage the second part of the great commandment as well—to "Love your neighbor as yourself" (Matthew 22:39). These people are some of the most loyal friends on earth because they are constantly looking for ways to strengthen relationships. They never utter an insincere compliment for the sake of appearing interested in others. Nor do they compliment others as a parenthetical insert in a rushed conversation. They are passionate about their marriage and do whatever is necessary to nurture it continually. They spend quality blocks of time with their children and invest liberally in their welfare.

Passionate about Work and Career

According to the Marketing and Research Corporation of Princeton, New Jersey, 50 to 80 percent of Americans are in the wrong job. Much of this chapter deals with the role of passion in our careers, which is a timely subject for millions of Americans who are unhappy with their work situation. It's hard to be passionate if you are misplaced.

Passionate about Everyday Living

Recently I watched some World War II footage about the liberation of Paris following the 1944 D day invasion. The Parisians had endured four long years of Nazi occupation. They were more than ready for liberation from the Allied forces. Originally, Eisenhower planned to bypass Paris and stay on schedule to crush Germany. However, after Eisenhower was persuaded enough Nazi firepower was left in Paris for considerable harm to both ancient structures and human life, he sent the Fourth Army to Paris. They cleaned up the pockets of German resistance. What a welcome these troops received! Some called it the greatest celebration in the history of the world. Tens of thousands of Parisians jammed the streets and showered the GIs with flowers and kisses. Many of the women had swollen faces from embracing so many stubbled American jaws.

Their celebration wasn't just one afternoon parade; it continued for days. They showed the world how to throw a party. The French have a great passion for life and for living. Nothing impassions them more than the fine art of food and drink.

The excesses from such a lifestyle are obvious. But there is something special, even spiritual, in observing the uninhibited dance of those with a zest for living.

What's Your Passion Personality?

Each one of us is different. We "have different motives, purposes, aims, values, needs, drives, impulses, urges. Nothing is more fundamental than that. [We] believe differently; [we] think, recognize, conceptualize, perceive, understand, comprehend, and cogitate differently. And of course, manners of acting and emoting, governed as they are by wants and beliefs, follow suit and differ radically among people."[1]

Over the years, many have tried to describe the varying temperaments that people have. Hippocrates described four possible personalities: sanguine, choleric, phlegmatic, and melancholic. Other descriptions have been adapted into personality tests such as the Myers-Briggs Type Indicator or the Kiersey Sorter, which describe a certain temperament's passion and how it might be expressed. Some personalities are motivated by being with other people, while others prefer pursuing quantifiable victories in their own lives. Another personality type spends time creating works of art or wrestling with great ideas.

No matter what type of personality you may have, passion always comes into play because it is the fuel for getting anything accomplished. Some people have a natural bent toward socializing, and they pursue a career in sales. But they still need a reason to get up every morning. Maybe they believe strongly in their product. Maybe they like the financial rewards from multiple sales. Whatever it is, these gifted salespeople need an internal motivator or passion to keep them on track. And when slothfulness drags like a dead weight and no one is checking to see how many hours they are putting in, they draw on this passion. Maybe the passion will be expressed through a fifteen-hour workday or from an emotional pep talk before a big event. Passion can be quiet or loud, visible or invisible, but it's there.

This force of passion is a great divider, separating the achievers from those content with mediocrity. It indicates that a person has a rudder on his or her boat. As Thomas Carlyle said, "Have a purpose in life, and having it, throw such strength of mind and muscle into your work as God has given you." The committed Christian eagerly looks for ways to implement whatever is needed to be a passionate person.

What Affects Our Passion?

Most people love lush green lawns. But in Florida, we have a problem with this—anything grows, but not everything green is good. I constantly battle crabgrass. It's green, makes a nice covering, and from a distance looks no different from grass sod. But crabgrass is a weed, and once it establishes a foothold, it will soon take over my yard.

To remove crabgrass takes radical treatment. At first I tried to mow it close to the ground so that the sun would scorch it out. Next I tried to pull it by hand. But I discovered crabgrass is like cancer. If one or two seeds are left in the soil, it returns. Only an all-out war will eliminate it. This weed has to be poisoned with chemicals that go to the roots. Several applications are necessary. If you try to ignore it or attack it only halfheartedly, it wins.

Like crabgrass, sin can also attack our passion. Through sin, our devotion to Christ, our service to others, our gifts, and our zest for living can be derailed and even extinguished. Many gifted people never reach their potential because they can't control the weeds of sin, such as power, money, sex, or drugs. Too often people dabble with these temptations. They are lulled into believing that if their weeds get too high or threatening, they can chop them down. Not so. Like demons, they have to be exorcised. And like the weeds in my lawn, sin comes in numerous categories. Every person knows the ones that are the most alluring eventually suck the life out of our commitment to Christ. While Christ followers aren't perfect, they don't like weeds in their lives. When they recognize one, they quickly move to see it eliminated.

Ten Requirements of Passionate People

Many practical lessons about leadership are found in Wess
Robert's *Leadership Secrets of Attila the Hun*. One of the most
basic requirements is an eagerness to lead. If people don't have
a passion to lead, they aren't going to be much use in the
corporate boardroom. This principle is true for any other
endeavor. Attila hypothetically was asked, "How, Attila, might
I know if I possess sufficient desire to be a chieftain?" Attila
was happy to offer his thoughts . . . some of which are the
same ten characteristics of passionate people.

#1: Remain True to Yourself

In order to remain true to yourself, you have to know yourself.
You have to discover your gifts, what God has called you to do,
and which roles you perform best. To some, this may sound
like a tall order to fill. But the discovery process is key to
unleashing our energies.

Most Christians know they have unique gifts. Paul said in
Romans, "We have different gifts, according to the grace given
us" (12:6) and "God's gifts and his call are irrevocable"
(11:29). If we are serious about our commitment to Christ, we
will take advantage of any of the various personality or gift
inventories. Through these inventories, we'll discover a pattern about our particular "bent," and we can celebrate the way
God made us.

There are two methods to get in touch with our gifts. One
avenue is to figure out our motivators—what we naturally
spend time on. Another mode is to pay attention to the compliments we receive. A friend of mine, Dick Hagstrom, has
helped me through the years by asking me about accomplishments that have brought a particular sense of fulfillment. I
went through this probing process—what Hagstrom calls a
"motivated ability pattern"—several times during various
stages of my career. Hagstrom picked out a pattern of experi-

ences I kept repeating. I learned it doesn't matter what type of job I have, I'll always try to express my gifts in a particular manner. If my job doesn't allow me this expression, then I'll perform the task in an uninspired way.

Some of the most frustrated people have many gifts, but they aren't sure which ones God wants them to employ. A man may have culinary gifts, but that doesn't mean, necessarily, he should be a chef. God wants us to use the gifts he has called us to use. Knowing which gifts to tap requires developing a listening ear to the voice of God. Then we need to determine whether we will obey once we understand his call. Oswald Chambers said, "If I hear the call of God and refuse to obey, I become the dullest, most common-place of Christians because I have seen and heard and refused to obey."

In order to receive our marching orders, it takes both a natural and logical understanding of how we are equipped, combined with the necessity of keeping close to God. Once our calling is obvious, we need to exercise our opportunities passionately. Paul said, "Whatever you do, work at it with all your heart, as working for the Lord, not for men, since you know that you will receive an inheritance from the Lord as a reward. It is the Lord Christ you are serving" (Colossians 3:23-24). Notice that Paul stated, "whatever you do." Paul didn't limit his words to *spiritual* activities; he spoke of *all* activities.

All of life is a spiritual responsibility. As the puritan John Cotton said, "A true believing Christian, a justified person, he lives in his vocation by his faith. Not only my spiritual life but even my civil life in this world, all the life I live, is by the faith of the Son of God: He exempts no life from the agency of His faith."

Later Cotton said that a calling could be summarized by: (1) The use of God-given gifts where God opened the door; (2) The faith that God would sharpen those useful gifts;

(3) The understanding that if he served God faithfully in his employment, then everyone would benefit, remembering "Serve wholeheartedly, as if you were serving the Lord, not men" (Ephesians 6:7); (4) Bringing dignity to whatever job he undertakes; (5) The trust that God is ultimately responsible for the success or failure; and (6) The knowledge that God doesn't ask you to stop your efforts until his work for you is accomplished.

After identifying our gifts and gaining a clear understanding of God's call, it helps to learn our particular role. Our role is a preference about our style of operation. For example, a person may be a gifted landscape architect. Because of his success, he quickly moves up in an organization and eventually manages other architects and spends the bulk of his time on company development. One day the architect realizes he's unhappy. He's not working in his preferred role, so he considers getting into another career, looking for another calling. Instead, all he really needs is a role adjustment and a return to the drawing board. Maybe his gifts are best used if he lets someone else manage the employees and company development.

To remain focused on our true role isn't selfish. If we are truly called by God, it's the only way to live. It prevents us from merely responding to whatever urges happen to be the most prevalent on any day.

#2: Be Willing to Prepare for Service

Those who are serious about their life's work and serving others want to be adequately prepared for the challenges ahead. They have a passion for learning and seek every opportunity for continuing education. These people agree with Cervantes, who said, "The man who is prepared has his battle half fought."

The apostle Paul was passionate about his duties as a Pharisee. He wrote the Galatians, "For you have heard of my previous way of life in Judaism, how intensely I persecuted the church of God and tried to destroy it. I was advancing in Judaism beyond many Jews of my own age and was extremely zealous for the traditions of my fathers" (Galatians 1:13-14).

After his conversion on the road to Damascus, Paul's intensity for learning switched to a desire that Christ would prepare him for service to his church. Paul lived in the desert for three years before returning to Jerusalem and beginning to contact the disciples.

In some ways, Paul's preparation reminds me of the decadent rock star of the 1970s and 1980s, Vincent Furnier, better known as Alice Cooper. Known for his gory concerts, which even had him hanging on a cross, Alice Cooper used to claim he was the reincarnation of a seventeenth-century witch. People who know Vincent Furnier report that he is now a devout follower of Christ. Like Paul, Furnier wants to prepare for service. After his conversion, Furnier wisely didn't go on television or the speaking circuit to tell about the change in his life. Instead, he began to study. He attended Ligonier conferences and listened to tapes by R. C. Sproul. His mind and his soul needed to be firmly grounded in the Scriptures. So quietly and without fanfare, he prepared for the long haul and not just his next stage appearance.

People who are prepared understand that life change can't be accomplished without discipline. Oftentimes, overcoming our emotions is the greatest struggle we face in accomplishing our goals. But as Pearl S. Buck said, "I don't wait for moods. You accomplish nothing if you do that. Your mind must know it has got to get down to earth."

Preparation isn't a lot of fun. It means setting aside the opportunity to be immediately on the battlefield. But passion fuels our desire to pay the necessary price to succeed.

#3: Be Willing to Make Personal Sacrifice—
Even When Unrecognized

It's a soft age in which we live. Discipline is still in vogue, but sacrifice is another matter. Churchill said, "I have nothing to offer but blood, toil, tears and sweat." Many in the twentieth century would agree with only portions of Churchill's statement—toil, tears, and sweat, but not blood. To them, sacrifice is the price paid by overzealous fools or someone not smart enough to get all the glory without having to fork over anything that costs personally.

Biblical role models paid a heavy price for their commitment. In order for Moses to follow God's will, he had to give up his position of security and prestige within Pharaoh's court. Then for forty years, he seemingly wasted away in the wilderness. Half of the people who knew Moses when he paid the price of obedience had died before he returned to Egypt. Few were left to pat Moses on the back for his personal sacrifice. His sojourn in the wilderness included the complete death of his dreams and the complete sacrifice of his relationships. However, it ultimately paid off in a dynamic relationship with God and a leadership role unequaled either before or since that time.

If you ask people to sacrifice for a cause, you'll discover their passion. But you may learn they're more interested in appearing disciplined than in offering real blood . . . the kind Churchill spoke about.

#4: Bounce Back from Personal
Discouragement and Rejection

As author M. Scott Peck said, "Life is difficult." There's nothing to clarify our vision like someone ridiculing our plans and casting aspersions on our sanity. In fact, it's probably impossible to accomplish anything of significance unless it has been severely challenged.

But difficulties are therapeutic. They clear the cobwebs out of our dreams and help us determine what we want. Problems are passion purifiers.

Several times in my life, I've dabbled at different tasks. For example, I enjoy silk-screen printing. I considered developing a part-time business that would print corporate decals for a vehicle fleet. It was a fun idea—until I realized the amount of commitment it would take to make it successful. That wasn't exactly what I had in mind. My passion wasn't there. It was a good idea, but it didn't go far. Only passionate ideas ultimately succeed.

If committed Christians face difficulties, they know the problems aren't terminal—that God is in charge. Take David for example, a man passionate about being God's follower. He didn't want to usurp the authority of his magistrate, Saul, but when the time was right, he wanted to be the best king Israel had ever seen. The Bible describes how David faced a lineup of problems longer than his ability to cope with them. He ended up hiding in caves and lived more like a desert jackal than the heir to the throne. Sometimes, in frustration, David couldn't figure out why everyone rejected him. On one occasion, David barely escaped with his life from Saul's armies and then sought refuge under the Philistine king, Achish of Gath. At first the Philistines saw a benefit in accepting this defector, but soon they realized David had a loyal following among the population of Israel.

King Achish apologizes to David, saying, "From the day you came to me until now, I have found no fault in you, but the rulers don't approve of you."

David replies, "But what have I done? . . . What have you found against your servant from the day I came to you until now?" (1 Samuel 29:6-8).

David fits the definition of the word *courage:* the mental

willingness to endure in spite of discouragement. He faced great difficulty, but he never gave up.

Those who are convinced they are doing God's work are overcomers even when it appears foolish to pursue their call passionately.

#5: Have the Ability to Focus and the Stamina to Follow Through

The inability to remain focused on our objectives is one of our greatest enemies—especially when other opportunities come our way. Bobb Biehl, from Masterplanning Group International, likens it to snow, which is composed of tiny flakes that can be held on your finger and examined for intricate structure. However, when snow falls rapidly and is driven by the wind, it becomes a blizzard—a whiteout. It transforms into danger. These millions of tiny flakes, blasting across the countryside in subfreezing temperatures, may remind us of our schedule. We feel overwhelmed, maybe even frozen in space and time, by a whiteout.

Those who attempt too many opportunities will probably have a difficult time unwinding on vacation. It will take several days for the snow to quit falling and for the mind to clear. Soon they realize that fatigue is more of a problem than they first thought. Their life is being dictated by everyone's agenda except their own. If they don't get control of their schedule, no quality time can be given to the things that matter most.

John Wesley pointed out this truth about staying focused: "Though I am always in haste, I am never in a hurry because I never undertake more work than I can go through with calmness of spirit." When you meet calm people, you admire their control. They don't flit from one place to another, from one topic of conversation to many. When they are with you, they are with you. These people approach every aspect of life in a deliberate fashion.

Jesus was the most focused person who ever walked the face

of the earth. When he was a child, his parents frantically looked for him after they left the temple in Jerusalem. But the experience taught Mary and Joseph a lesson. For Jesus, there was no question of priorities: His Father's business came first. When it was time for him to start his public ministry, Christ focused on a limited audience, the wayward sons of Israel. His message was narrow: "The kingdom of God is near. Repent and believe the Good News." Although his time was short, Jesus understood the importance of withdrawing to a mountain in order to recharge for his mission. He was passionate about staying on target—nothing could stop him.

It's easy for mediocrity to creep into our lives. We all need to have a constant "reality check" regarding our schedule. People who know us best and understand our gifts and passions need to know what's logged in our Day-Timer. They can protect us from the blizzard and allow us to focus, once again, on God's unique design.

#6: Be Creative in Endeavors

Every gift has its own realm of creativity. Some are quite obvious, such as art, acting, or architecture. The final products are there for everyone to observe. Immediately the trained eye sees whether the final product was fueled by passion. This visibility is also true in fields less known for creative ventures, such as the sales field. Most think there are two approaches: hard sell and soft sell. But those who are really good at sales study every nuance and make a fine art of knowing when and how to say the right thing that sparks the buyer's interest.

The same holds true for management. A good manager used to be evaluated on his or her ability to create an efficient workforce and to put out a product with minimum frustrations and maximum productivity in the shortest amount of time. However, passionate managers became creative. They learned what internally motivated their employees. Efficiency couldn't be measured in short bursts; often people broke down if they were under too much pressure and had too little understanding of their working conditions. The most productive managers were those with two additional qualities: compassionate understanding of the rigors of the working environment and some level of ownership in the profitability of the company.

Often the most gifted workers want to be creative, but creativity is impossible without at least the following three ingredients:

Time to think. Creativity requires hours, sometimes days, before the quality begins to flow. The mind needs to be free from pressure and the competition of television, radio, or telephone. Our social agenda needs to be on neutral. I personally experience my greatest flow of creativity when I get away to the Colorado Rockies. The change of scenery, the refreshing summer climate, and the beauty of mountains and lakes is a tonic hard to duplicate.

Physical refreshment. Creativity and fatigue don't mix; we need nourishment. When running for his life from Queen Jezebel, Elijah collapsed, exhausted, beside a broom tree. "'I have had enough, Lord,' he said. 'Take my life; I am no better than my ancestors'" (1 Kings 19:4). An accompanying angel didn't give Elijah a lecture on being a quitter. Instead, the angel allowed him to sleep, then made sure he ate some solid meals.

While we may not be "on the run" for our life, like Elijah, we also can lose our bearings and want to hang it up. Only negative thoughts can flow in a time like that.

Good thoughts. Creativity needs not only physical nourishment but also a nurturing environment. It doesn't flow when we are worried, afraid, or agitated. A troubled mind isn't a creative mind because the passion to excel is replaced by a fight to regain mental equilibrium.

In one of Paul's last exhortations to the Philippians, he said,

"Finally, brothers, whatever is true, whatever is noble, whatever is right, whatever is pure, whatever is lovely, whatever is admirable—if anything is excellent or praiseworthy—think about such things" (4:8). This may be one of the most powerful admonitions in Scripture. It's not about a prudish lifestyle but about mental survival and unblocking our flow of creativity that invigorates the world. By following Paul's admonition, we can go to sleep thinking new thoughts instead of battling hellish memories that could have been avoided.

Good thoughts are also empowered by the verbal encouragement of others, especially those who influence us. Supervisors should realize their ability to empower the workforce with words that are noble, right, pure, lovely, and admirable. Such words are fuel to launch a thousand shuttles.

#7: Be Willing to Exaggerate Your Cause

At first, this characteristic sounds suspicious because it seems like boasting. However, when you believe in something strongly, it's hard to contain the enthusiasm. No doubt every passionate person uses a little hyperbole at one time or another. Various people in Scripture were quite good at exaggeration. When David said, "I will walk in my house with blameless heart. I will set before my eyes no vile thing," he meant, "Because of my love for you, Lord, I'll do my best to keep short accounts with you and to check what I see and read" (Psalm 101:2-3).

Some people exaggerate because they have low self-esteem, and exaggerating gains attention. For others, exaggerations are the overspill of enthusiasm about their cause. For example, the promotional brochure for a nationally based ministry says their objective is to cause a spiritual awakening in America. Wouldn't we all like to say that's our goal? But I'm not going to check on this ministry—and its leader—in two years to see how near we are to such an awakening. The leader is so passionate about seeing people come to Christ and encouraging racial reconciliation that he has put into print the burden that flames inside him.

Believers who print such brochures aren't worried about my perspective on their mission. They aren't looking for permission but rather for results. Passionate people aren't trying to win popularity contests; they're trying to fulfill their dreams. (Unfortunately, the danger always exists that some aren't exaggerating. They're just lying simpletons who are energized by blind zeal. These zealots give a bad reputation to passionate people.)

Passionate people have overcome a key problem—a personal sense of inadequacy or shyness. Only bold people hyperbolize. When God called Jeremiah to be a prophet to Judah, Jeremiah responded with less than zealous agreement. "Ah, Sovereign Lord . . . I do not know how to speak; I am only a child" (Jeremiah 1:6). Those who say "I am only . . ." lack passion or are in search of affirmation. God wanted Jeremiah to say, "I may be only . . . but look what we can accomplish together." That's divine affirmative action.

#8: Have the Burning Desire to Succeed

Passion for passion's sake isn't much good. Passion must have a target. Ultimately, the desire is to succeed, to be victorious. The Bible is loaded with success language spoken by, and on behalf of, some of its most famous characters.

Unfortunately, some people believe *success* is a dirty word. My own hunch is that these people are unwilling to risk failure or to admit they will have setbacks. But these failures and setbacks are often the building blocks to a larger understanding of God's will. Those who don't have dreams to shoot for are free from the agonies of not accomplishing something that is very important to them. But they miss the joy of answered prayers and the close relationship that a committed Christian can have with God.

#9: Do Not Be Threatened by Talented Contemporaries

Poor King Saul. The Israelites sang, "Saul has slain his thousands, and David his tens of thousands" (1 Samuel 18:7) and the monarch was completely undone. Saul's downfall is always attributed to his duplicitous nature (wanting to obey God and be a good king, while still acting however he pleased) or his fits of jealousy.

If passionate people aren't jealous people, then Saul's real problem was his lack of single-mindedness. That's the problem duplicitous people deal with: the inability to take a stand. They get moving in one direction, the creativity flows, and their enthusiasm builds until they are distracted. Their passion drains from one agenda and begins to build toward another. In the meantime, when they see someone else making great progress in one area, and passionately so, they become jealous.

Instead of wasting their time and energy on jealousy, passionate people are *challenged* by capable contemporaries. They want to learn the secrets that others have employed to make such enormous strides. They want to be controlled by the discipline of a focused objective, not by emotional outbursts because of the success of others.

When we feel threatened by someone's achievements, we need to do three things: First, thank God for their success; second, personally congratulate them; third, ask the Lord to give us a single passion. Once that match of passion is lit, we won't have the time to be jealous about what others accomplish!

#10: Be Willing to Work on Your Flaws

When a critic asked Billy Graham about a particular rumor of a weakness in his ministry, he responded, "I've got weaknesses you don't even know about. Do you want me to list those for you?" Now that's a disarming reply!

David, the "man after God's own heart," didn't battle rages of jealousy as King Saul did. But he had other problems to deal with. No one knew better than David that he had character flaws, and he didn't try to hide them: "For I know my transgressions, and my sin is always before me" (Psalm 51:3). Then, like a marine sergeant looking for dust, David invited God to inspect his life: "Search me, O God, and know my heart; test me and know my anxious thoughts. See if there is any offensive way in me, and lead me in the way everlasting" (Psalm 139:23-24).

Passionate people are willing to look for personal flaws because they don't want to deceive themselves. A flaw doesn't have to be a sin; it can be a character defect. Maybe it's difficult for us to listen to others. If people are turned off because we don't know how to listen, this flaw may ultimately damage our ability to attain our goals. If we are serious about using every resource to be successful, we may have to admit that we treat people rudely when they are talking. We also have to be willing to ask for help.

Passionate people know they need others, and they need their honesty and encouragement, too.

From time to time, we all experience one of the greatest passion killers—disillusionment. A friend of mine in Texas has battled an aching disillusionment for years. One of his best friends decided to give him the cold shoulder and withdraw from their relationship—permanently. With a hole in his heart, this friend continues to identify his passion and moves on. Although he struggles, he refuses to let anything ultimately derail him from reaching his goals.

The Bottom Line

How do you identify your passion? First, *find the things you constantly think about.* Ask yourself, *What local, global, social, or religious issues stir me emotionally?*

Leonard Rodgers, the founder of Venture Middle East, has tremendous compassion for poor and disadvantaged people in places like Lebanon and Egypt. During the long and tortuous civil war in Beirut, Leonard risked his life to bring supplies to people who were suffering immeasurably. He organized relief efforts to provide medical supplies and nurses to bind the wounds of the Kurds after the Gulf War. More recently, he has launched a campaign called "Family to Family" to give people in the West an opportunity to help feed or clothe another family in the Middle East for one month. There's never a doubt about Leonard's passion, and that kind of passion is contagious.

Second, *ask what you would do with your life if you knew you couldn't fail.* Sometimes passion is hard to figure out because dreams have been suppressed for a long time. What used to excite you?

Sometimes people are so afraid that they will never have the opportunity to fulfill those dreams or that they would fail if given the chance. So what do they do? They make a conscious choice not to live with the pain of unfulfilled longings. Instead of praying for an open door or the courage to step out at a golden moment, they shoot the dream in the heart. But dreams are intricately connected to people. And when dreams die, people are severely wounded in the process.

I heard a man from Missouri once say, "God uses desperate people." By that he meant desperate people are passionate people. They accomplish much because they refuse to give up. Passion can take its toll in lost sleep. It can add wear and tear to the body. But passionate people will tell you they are fortunate people because they believe strongly in something. When committed Christians leave their comfort zones, they can't do it without the fuel of passion.

THINKING IT THROUGH

1. What are you passionate about? Give several examples.

2. How do you think your personality affects your passion?

3. What is your biggest obstacle in keeping your passion focused? Why?

4. Look up the following verses. What do they have to say about passion?

- Numbers 25:10-13
- Proverbs 19:2
- John 2:17
- Romans 12:6-8, 11
- Galatians 4:18

5. What environment best nurtures your passion? How can you build that environment into your life more often?

6. Of the ten requirements for passionate people, which one do you struggle with the most? Why? As you pray this week, ask God to help you work on that "requirement" so you can become more passionate for him.

8

Practice Humility

There are three great motives that urge us to humility. It strengthens me as a man, as a sinner, and as a saint.

ANDREW MURRAY

THE television series *Roots* garnered tremendous success. Not only did it trace the history of native Africans from slave ships to the cotton plantations of the American South, it sent a million viewers to libraries and courthouses in search of their own heritage. My family was among those curious searchers.

Like everyone else, we wondered if there was anyone famous in our family tree. Our investigation was rewarding, not because we recognized some names from American history that were distantly linked to the Kreider name, but because of one particularly interesting story.

Most of the Kreider ancestors, as German Mennonites, sailed to America at the request of William Penn, who generously offered two thousand acres of land (now called Germantown) near Philadelphia. King Charles II had granted this property to William Penn on March 4, 1681, so the people could live religiously as they wished, without restraint from England's government.

One set of relatives, the Cassel family, emigrated from Kriesheim, Germany, in 1686 on the ship *Jefries*. As Mennonites, they enjoyed the simple approach to everyday life and worship. They were known for their plainness of dress, their frugality, and their honesty. Not long after they settled into the New World, this lifestyle received its greatest test.

One day they received a letter from Europe, telling them a wealthy relative had died and left a large estate, worth nearly a million dollars. They only had to return to Europe to accept the money.

A church council was called to discuss the matter. After a free and lively discussion, the people took a vote about whether they thought the Cassels should accept the offer. The unanimous decision was to refuse. The reason? Money has a tendency to make people proud!

I had to read this story several times to grasp the issues my ancestors struggled with because rejecting money for humility's sake is so foreign to our twentieth-century culture. Basically, this group of people, who lived in relative poverty, had turned down the comparable equivalent of over a billion dollars—just so they could remain humble!

These days, humility isn't exactly a hot sermon topic or book theme. If you go to a local Christian bookstore to see how many books are available on this theme, you'll be hard-pressed to locate even chapters or paragraphs that are dedicated to this characteristic. Apparently humility has little reader appeal and isn't much of a marketable commodity. But it *is* an important characteristic of a committed Christian, primarily because so many people—even Christians—are arrogantly consumed with themselves. Jesus spent a great deal of time discussing the virtue of humility; it was one of the crowning characteristics of the life of Christ.

To be honest, I didn't want to write about humility because it's a difficult subject to grasp. Yet, although I tried, I couldn't set it aside. And, as I studied Scripture and examined two classics on the subject, *Humility* by Andrew Murray and *The Steps of Humility* by Bernard of Clairvaux (a twelfth-century monk), I discovered that humility is critically intertwined with the other characteristics of a committed Christian.

Can a person have passion, be driven to accomplish great things for God, and at the same time remain humble? The answer is a resounding yes. In the following pages, we'll examine nine thoughts about this characteristic of humility.

What Is Humility?
Most dictionaries describe *humility* by discussing the opposite characteristics—arrogance and pride. The Greeks called pride *hubris,* a trait that appeared often in the tragic heroes of Greek literature. This trait meant a total disregard for the limits governing men's actions. It was overconfidence, and the Greek gods found it offensive. It was an attempt to bypass mortality.

The statues of famous Greek generals are a lasting memorial to the glory of accomplishment and the triumph over enemies; they are also a testimony to arrogant people who were so preoccupied with themselves that they failed to see the need to bow their knee to anyone. If they had bowed in humility, they would have admitted their lack of self-sufficiency and their need of someone else to help them navigate issues regarding eternity.

Although a key element of humility is recognizing our weaknesses, this doesn't mean we attempt to mutilate our self-respect or destroy our ego. Jesus didn't have a "dump on me, I'm a garbage heap" mentality. He had enormous inner strength and an identity that was completely intact.

Thomas Merton said, "Humility that freezes our being and frustrates all healthy activity is not humility at all, but a disguised form of pride." Humility can't be equated only with meditation and contemplation. Through her tireless efforts, Mother Teresa has shown us that humble people are often very active. They know their gifts and have identified the passion of their soul.

Truly humble people acknowledge that they are human, frail, and prone to evil and deception. But they also know that God is merciful, willing to offer freedom and strength to those who seek his honor and not their own. Oswald Chambers called humility "the great characteristic of the saint." I consider it the mother of all virtues.

Humility ≠ Humiliation

An Indian proverb says, "To give dignity to man is above all things." I learned this proverb from Jim, a man who began experimenting with heroin in Vietnam and subsequently battled drug abuse for many years. In order to see what would become of Jim, a television reporter maintained tabs on him during this time of addiction. Although Jim was very bright, he was out of control. Internally, he knew he had the ability to make something out of his life. But he also knew, despite the embarrassment, that he needed a heroin fix—even if it meant mainlining on national television.

After many years of attempted rehabilitation and numerous self-help programs, Jim finally kicked the habit and went to work. Now he is a wealthy man and runs his own business. He is very aware that he wouldn't have made it if some people hadn't been committed to pulling him out of his humiliation.

Humiliation is the fallout of lowered dignity. Whatever the

circumstance, the victim is usually embarrassed. *Humility* is a garment that a person puts on willingly; *humiliation* is forced on another person. When the apostle Peter denied his Lord three times, he went away and wept bitterly. Why? Peter had sinned. Only a few hours earlier, he had boasted of his loyalty to Jesus; now he didn't have the resolve to follow through. Sin does that; it often sets a trap where the only way out is public disgrace.

Humiliation isn't always bad. When Chuck Colson was imprisoned after his conviction for participating in the Watergate cover-up, his humiliation led not only to repentance but to one of the most influential testimonies in the country. The man who led Chuck to Christ fulfilled the Indian proverb. He restored a man's dignity.

Humble people have their dignity intact. They are aware of the areas where they have gifts and gratefully acknowledge others who admire or compliment their work. They don't try to wear a garment of false humility. They want to glorify God in everything, including how their skills are used. If they draw ill-timed or awkward attention to the fact they are nothing and God deserves all the credit, then the attention shifts to their inability to graciously accept a compliment instead of encouraging others to glorify God.

Those who have been humiliated in a public setting for not measuring up to expectations will often try even more diligently to convince others about their talent. But people who are truly humble won't parade or flaunt their gifts.

Humility in the Life of Jesus

One of the most important passages about humility is Paul's description of how humility was exhibited in the life of Jesus:

163

> Do nothing out of selfish ambition or vain conceit, but in humility consider others better than yourselves. Each of

you should look not only to your own interests, but also to the interests of others. Your attitude should be the same as that of Christ Jesus: Who, being in very nature God, did not consider equality with God something to be grasped, but made himself nothing, taking the very nature of a servant, being made in human likeness. And being found in appearance as a man, he humbled himself and became obedient to death—even death on a cross! Therefore God exalted him to the highest place and gave him the name that is above every name. *Philippians 2:3-9*

Three important words stand out from these verses. The first is *grasped.* Jesus modeled humility by releasing his grip. To join the human race, Christ gave up his rights to remain seated at the right hand of the Father. Andrew Murray called humility "Man's simple consent to let go" (a similar concept to what we discussed in chapter 1, on yielding control). Jesus also let go, knowing in advance that his life would end in death. That's a lot tougher than not knowing the outcome or believing yielding will result in something beneficial.

Think about this: Christ chose to become a man, not an angel. Angels could only come with curiosity. But a man could come with sympathy because he was acquainted with human misery. By not grasping his rights, Jesus became "a man of sorrows, and familiar with suffering" (Isaiah 53:3). Jesus made himself accessible to those who needed a refuge when their world collapsed around them (Hebrews 4:15-16). Through following the example of Jesus, we allow God to position us to provide hope wherever God sees fit. One thing is certain: Unless we ourselves are wounded, we won't be much use to anyone. (We'll deal with that topic in-depth in the next chapter.)

The second important word in the Philippians passage is *nothing.* Jesus exchanged the royal position of heaven to become a servant—a lowly position in the eyes of the world. Jesus completely reduced his status. He laid aside or released all his trappings of honor and influence.

One of my favorite stories to illustrate this kind of downsizing comes from Steve Douglass, the executive vice president of Campus Crusade for Christ.

Steve graduated from MIT with a degree in engineering, then went on to earn his MBA from Harvard. Everyone expected him to accomplish great things in business. But Steve decided to pursue a career in ministry—he knew he was called to evangelism.

Since he ranked in the upper percentile of his graduating class at Harvard, Steve was invited to a special dinner where fourteen seniors told the faculty and administration about their goals for life. One student told of his plans to work for one of the finest consulting firms in the world. Another announced his recent appointment to a high position in one of the largest U.S. industries.

Finally they listened to Steve Douglass. He announced, "I've decided to go to work for Campus Crusade for Christ." The reaction from the audience was total disbelief and a pregnant pause. Steve says, "There were coughs, forks dropped, eyes averted, not able to watch what was happening. I could almost read their minds, *Where have we gone wrong?*" There was no honor or prestige in the fact that one of Harvard's finest would be earning five thousand dollars a year. In fact, they discounted Steve's salary when they calculated the average statistics for their graduates. Steve had released his hold on the trappings of wealth and honor. In the eyes of his peers and institutional leaders he was a nothing.

The third important word that describes Christ's humility is *Obedient . . . obedient to death.* Releasing isn't really releasing, reduction in status isn't really reduction unless it means absolute, unequivocal obedience to do what God asks. For

Jesus, it meant death. When Peter asked Jesus about what obedience meant for the apostle John, Jesus said; "If I want him to remain alive until I return, what is that to you? You must follow me" (John 21:22). In other words, "Mind your own business, Peter." Obedience will require different things for different people. But no humility will be achieved without this type of obedience.

Humility: What Does It Mean for Us?

First, it means we pattern our lives after Christ as much as possible. We follow in his steps. Second, we discover how a humble person feels in the presence of God. When we are really humble, we realize we have volunteered for service, much like a new army recruit who awaits orders from the commander-in-chief. More than likely, we will feel like a pauper, not because we are a poor little waif, but because we are now in a situation where wealth is meaningless. A new recruit in the armed forces receives only government issue—those belongings the government believes to be important. The humble person is only concerned with what is issued or deemed important by his heavenly Commander. All the things that matter most in this life, like wealth, power, position, and influence, are inconsequential to those who humbly follow Christ. These Christians have pledged loyalty to his kingdom.

We will feel inadequate in the presence of God—not in a morbid sense like a grub that deserves to be squashed, but like a fireman trying to put out a three-story blaze with a sand pail. Against such overwhelming odds, we are completely helpless.

Third, we will need to give up our thirst for independence. Dependence on God will be a hallmark of our lives. Like the firefighter with the sand pail, we open ourselves to receive God's strength in helpless situations. We begin to understand that our dilemmas need divine wisdom and that ultimately our dependence is an experience of freedom. If the sand pail isn't sufficient, then God will have to provide other equipment so the job can be completed.

Fourth, humility impacts the way we treat others. When others succeed, we rejoice. When the opportunity arises, we elevate others while slipping into the shadows ourselves. When others are in pain, we let ourselves be touched by their sorrow. Andrew Murray called this our "true nobility."

What Did Jesus Teach?

Jesus talked many times about humility, presenting it as a foundational principle for the Christian life. Jesus had no need to sell books; he wasn't looking to be a guest rabbi on national television in Israel. Instead, he was interested in providing his disciples with five keys to unlock an authentic relationship with himself and provide the fulcrum to move the world. What are those keys?

Key #1. The kingdom belongs to those who realize they have nothing to offer. These people are poor in spirit and meek, but one day they'll be rewarded (Matthew 5:3, 5).

Key #2. Only as you follow the humble example of Christ will you find rest for your soul (Matthew 11:29).

Key #3. A child is the greatest example of a hero in heaven. Children are completely dependent and completely content to let God be everything (Matthew 18:4).

Key #4. The only way up is down. Pursue honor, and you'll lose it. Pursue humility, and you'll be exalted (Luke 14:11).

Key #5. Humility isn't just an attitude, it's an action. It will find ways of expressing itself (John 13:14).

The Disciples: Models of Humility?

On several occasions, the disciples revealed their true colors to Jesus. Although they had walked with him for months, listening to his instructions, they had heard very little. Spiritual teaching didn't conquer their pride. Often it elevated their emotional temperature without producing obedience to what is really important.

Consider the experience on the Mount of Transfiguration. Peter, James, and John had the ultimate ghost encounter. They saw Jesus take on the radiance of heaven while Moses and Elijah observed. Peter was so excited as a result of the experience that he wanted to erect a monument.

But the memory of this spiritual milestone didn't even have time to cool before the disciples began to argue about which one was the greatest. So much for humility. It wasn't going to happen—at least not while Jesus was with them. They needed his presence in them. Christ would have to die for them to internalize his teaching.

Humility requires supernatural strength, as the apostle John learned when he said, "The one who is in you is greater than the one who is in the world" (1 John 4:4). John knew what he was talking about. He and the rest of the disciples were recovering ego addicts. None of them would transform their lives without a power greater than their arrogance.

Six Principles of a Humble Person

What principles characterize a humble person? There are six: admitting personal limitations, seeking the will of God, not seeking worldly honor, not promoting self, seeking to serve others, yielding complete control. We'll examine each in turn.

Principle #1: Admit Personal Limitations (John 5:19)

Not long ago Ed Diaz spoke to a Gathering of Men Bible study about how to be a good father. He practices what he preaches. Although he is the director for Search Ministries in Central Florida and the baseball coordinator for the Detroit Tigers chapel program, Ed says his real full-time job is raising four boys.

Ed taught some practical lessons about how fathering was

the number-one responsibility for a man—even exceeding career aspirations. A key principle, Ed believes, is the importance of not losing your temper—even when circumstances justify it. Here's an example of that from his own life.

One hot and muggy summer afternoon Ed's four boys were working on their lawn. One mowed, one edged, one used the weed eater, and another raked. Then an argument flared between the two youngest boys. Before it could be stopped, a fight broke out. The youngest got punched in the face a couple of times, and Ed's anger rose faster than his rationality. "Do you want to see how this feels?" Ed yelled, grabbing the aggressor and landing a blow to his stomach. Suddenly he realized what he had done. Previously he had promised never to physically punish a boy after age thirteen. Now he had violated his promise and felt awful. He asked his son for forgiveness.

The overriding lesson for me as I heard Ed's story was that I can't always do what I know is right. In our attempt to be perfect parents, we *are* limited. We need help—and, more often, we need forgiveness.

A proud man couldn't have told that story because prideful people always want to appear as if they have their act together; to these people, limitations are a sign of weakness. But there are four boys in central Florida who know that's not true. Instead, they greatly admire their dad for his vulnerability.

Principle #2: Seek the Will of God (John 6:38)
Anyone who reads the Gospels with an open mind will probably be impressed with the leadership qualities of Jesus. These qualities are transferable from age to age and from culture to culture. They describe aspects of Christ's goal orientation, his resoluteness, and his concern for his associates. This same reader might see Christ's final confrontation with hypocritical Jewish leaders as the culmination of his efforts and the D day

of his destiny, which unfortunately led to his arrest and execution.

But anyone who reads the Gospels and misses John 6:38 misses the whole point. Jesus came to do the will of his Father. He wasn't goal-oriented, he was God-oriented. His heavenly Father led him into a no-win conflict with the chief priests of the Sanhedrin. His Father led him to stand before Pilate. His Father led him to a jagged cliff called the "place of the skull." Jesus didn't have to follow, but he did because following God was the motivation of his life.

The humble pray, "Thy will be done," just like Jesus. Although they don't always understand their situation, they know they don't have a better way to live.

Principle #3: Don't Seek Worldly Honor (John 5:41)

Flattery is a sticky web. Each of us is drawn to its lure, but a little is never enough. After a while we repeat the act that attracted the praise because it feels so good. Soon we can predict when it will come. We have been seduced into a life that is void of a pure motive.

To humiliate someone for offering a sincere compliment or for honoring our accomplishments isn't the answer. Humble people aren't insensitive—they'll quietly accept the gratuity without making a scene. But they can live without the praise. In fact, they prefer to live without it because they know honor is a narcotic that ravages its victims. The only applause they seek is from the One who has the authority to say, "Well done, good and faithful servant! Enter into the joy of your master" (Matthew 25:21, paraphrased).

Principle #4: Don't Promote Yourself (John 8:50)

I know a man who was given the chance to write a book. He had thought about writing for many years. As a child, he remembered occasionally taking a pad of paper and a pencil and experimenting with paragraphs. But then his life took on other priorities, like marriage and children, and the years rolled on. While his kids were growing up and his job was so demanding, he never had the time to spare. Then one day he was asked to write a chapter. The publisher thought the chapter was acceptable, and the man was given several other opportunities to teach on the subject of the chapter.

He felt he would always be a man of chapters, not books. Then, during one eight-hour stretch of driving, a book came to him. As he fumbled for a notepad in his door side panel, he began to jot down the outline. The thoughts kept him occupied, and the eight hours passed like eight minutes.

This man also had a knack for promotion. He thought about different people to call, organizations to contact, and ways of positioning his new creation. Unfortunately, such promotional efforts violated some of the most important principles he taught in his book. When he wrote about humility, he realized the ground under him wasn't secure. So he wrote about concepts that were painful reminders of his own pride.

Since I am this man, I proceed with a writing limp . . . a constant reminder of my frailties.

Principle #5: Seek to Serve Others (Luke 22:26-27)

Sometimes silence teaches more than talking. Notice what Jesus didn't say to his disciples as they discussed the litmus test for greatness for the second time—this time during the Last Supper. Jesus doesn't say, "Seek to impress others." No one is ever impressed into the kingdom. He doesn't say, "Go capture enemy-held territory." Such advances are nearly always tentative. He doesn't say, "Sharpen your gifts." Greatness is about character, not skills.

The biggest mistake many Christians make is trying to become a full-blown servant overnight. It's like trying to lift a two-hundred-pound weight without any previous workout.

We may succeed, but it's so painful we can't use those muscles again for a while. We have to ease into humility. We have to continue with the program long enough to establish a habit. We have to discover our maximum weight. Through experimentation, we learn when to take a break from routine and recuperate.

Serving others isn't like taking bad medicine. While it may be an acquired taste, it doesn't require much to be satisfying. The joy we bring to others is the payoff. When we wanted to begin a 7 A.M. Bible study for men in Winter Park, Florida, Jim, the acting rector at the time, said, "Don't worry about the food. The church will handle everything. They can prepare and serve it." He didn't mention that the pastoral staff would be the servants. When five episcopal priests donned aprons, served breakfast, and enjoyed it immensely, the eighty-seven men at the study learned a great lesson that morning about humility (even though it wasn't the topic of our lesson).

Principle #6: Yield Complete Control

Although we addressed this principle in an earlier chapter, a reminder doesn't hurt. Yielding control is so important to the committed Christian life, and many obstacles prevent it from happening. But one thing is certain: We can't be humble, yielding servants if we always need to dominate, to be top dog, to know everything. Such people often get their way because most people want to get out of their way.

Being Humble: What an Advantage!

The new term that defines an individual's persona is *attitude*. If a person storms into his house after work, then vents anger on the first human or animal that crosses his path, this man has an *attitude*. Unfortunately, it's a hostile attitude.

On two occasions in the New Testament, Jesus was impressed with an attitude. Once was with the centurion in

Matthew 8:5-13. This military official was used to being in control—in control of his soldiers and probably the majority of the things that came his way in life. But he couldn't heal his young servant. When Jesus offered to go to his village and heal the boy, the centurion kindly objected. As a man who was accustomed to giving orders, then expecting them to be followed without debate or delay, he humbly declared his personal sense of inadequacy and said to Jesus, "Just say the word, and my servant will be healed."

Jesus was astounded. Even the religious leaders of Israel wouldn't have suggested such a thing. They would have insisted on traveling to the home, anointing the child with ceremonial oil, and following through with the rabbinical teachings on dealing with the infirmed.

Jesus seemed to suggest that the faith of the centurion was as rare as a spiritually genuine Pharisee. This man's attitude of humility was synonymous with faith. The result? The sick boy was healed, and the centurion was exalted. Being exalted is the reward of humility. Just listen to what Jesus says in Luke 14:11: "For everyone who exalts himself will be humbled, and he who humbles himself will be exalted."

On another occasion, a Canaanite woman pleaded with Jesus for his touch on her demon-possessed daughter. This was one of those annoying situations that got under the skin of the disciples. Their attitude was "Get rid of her . . . she's bugging us."

When Jesus told the Gentile woman his mission was to the Jews, not to the Gentiles, his words should have stopped her persistent request for help. But she prostrated herself, falling to her knees as an act of complete submission and humility. Then Jesus turned to her and said something that, on the surface, sounded very strange: "It is not right to take the children's bread and toss it to their dogs" (Matthew 15:26). By saying this, he was pointing out the attitude of the Jews, who considered the Gentiles to be dogs. In essence, Jesus was creating a situation where she could either respond in faith or return dejected to her family. Also, Jesus made it clear that he reflected the common Jewish sentiment—that only the Jews deserved the blessings of God.

The lady's response impressed Jesus. She said she would gladly be called anything, even a dog, if that's what it took to taste any leftover blessings after the Jews got their fill. Such humility! Jesus said it smelled of faith, and it was an aroma that led to her daughter's healing.

Each of these two stories about Jesus and humility involved people outside of the official religious club. They illustrated to a Jewish world what humility looked like. The message was clear: If these nonkosher, uncircumcised heathen could be exalted for displaying such great humility, then no one on earth is exempt from the same opportunity.

The Bottom Line
If you wish to pursue a humble lifestyle in order to become a committed Christian, how can you begin? The following steps can be life changing.

- First, admit your sinfulness to God.
- Then pray (you may want to try kneeling).
- Ask for forgiveness if you have wronged someone.
- Seek counseling or ask a trusted friend for a listening ear.
- Ask the leaders of your church to pray for you.
- Invite your closest friends over for a time of prayer.
- List in a journal your feelings and thoughts about God. For instance, *I don't feel worthy of his love; how can he really care about me after all I've done?*

If you pursue even one of the above options, you are on

your way to becoming a humble person—a person "after God's own heart"—who can make a tremendous difference in the world.

THINKING IT THROUGH

1. Have you ever seen a false display of public humility? If so, give an example (without naming the person).

2. Look up the following verses. What do they say about humility?

   - 2 Chronicles 7:14
   - Psalm 25:9
   - Psalm 149:4
   - Proverbs 11:2
   - Isaiah 66:2
   - Philippians 2:3-9
   - Colossians 2:18
   - 1 Peter 5:5-6

3. What characteristics of our culture make it difficult to be humble? Why?

4. Is there a difference between being *goal-oriented* and being *God-oriented?* Do you think you can be both, or are they mutually exclusive? Why?

5. What do you hold on to? How does that affect your level of humility?

6. When you hear the word *humble,* what people spring to mind? Describe the traits that make them humble.

7. Are you truly a humble person? Why or why not? If not, what can you do to develop the characteristic of humility in your life?

9

Turn Tragedy into an Investment

*When our souls lie barren in a winter which seems hopeless
and endless, God has not abandoned us. His work goes on.
He asks our acceptance of the painful process and our trust
that He will indeed give resurrection life.*

ELISABETH ELLIOT

OUR family met the Furley family during the mid-1970s
when we helped begin a new church in Quail Valley, a suburb
southwest of Houston. I'm not sure where Edmund got the
nickname "Beaver," but it stuck. One day the whole family
showed up at church: Beaver, his wife, Gina, and their four
boys, Norman, Jonathan, Daniel, and David.

During the boom years of the Texas economy, Beaver had
done very well in residential real estate. They had a beautiful
home nestled under oak and pecan trees, which they gladly

offered for church use. It became the site for Easter egg hunts, Bible studies, baptisms in the Jacuzzi, high school parties, and Fourth of July picnics. Although certain events took their toll on their property, the Furleys continued to make their home available in gratitude to God for all he had done in their lives.

One dark night, in 1984, their world caved in. As they traveled a lonely road thirty miles west of Austin, Texas, on their way to Marble Falls for a visit with Gina's family, a drunk college student slammed into their car. Nine-year-old Jonathan was thrown out the back window. When the car finally quit spinning and came to a stop, Beaver jumped out into the black night and frantically looked for him. Only moments before the accident, Jonathan had been asleep in the backseat, and Beaver desperately wanted to find his son still sleeping. But deep inside he knew that just wasn't going to happen. Finally, in the glow of the one remaining headlight, Beaver spotted Jonathan.

Beaver said, "As I sat on the cold ground and pulled my son Jonathan to my lap, I saw the damage to his sweet face. I knew that damage would never be repaired."

As Beaver returned to his car, he saw that other family members were hurt, too. Daniel had severe head injuries. Gina had a ruptured eyeball, a hip and pelvis broken in three places, a bruised heart, and a collapsed lung. An undiagnosed ruptured spleen nearly took her life.

During the next several years, Beaver went through several career gyrations. Eventually he went full-time with Grace Ministries, a counseling center in Atlanta, and there began to help people cope with pain. He relearned the same lessons about pain over and over as his family moved from one crisis to another.

When I saw Beaver, he told me about another chapter in the ongoing saga. "Let's fast-forward about eight years. It's a few days after Christmas, and my fourteen-year-old is outside, putting his bicycle in the back of the car. I'm getting ready to take him to a friend's home."

Suddenly their home was filled with panicky screams. "Dad, help! Dad, come quick!" Beaver burst into his kitchen and found Daniel, a look of fear frozen on his face as his body writhed in a massive seizure. Beaver grabbed Daniel in a big bear hug, partly to make sure he didn't fall, partly hoping that if he squeezed tightly enough, whatever was broken would disappear.

Six hours later, Beaver learned the problem wouldn't go away. "Your son has a brain tumor," the doctor said quietly as he looked at the CAT-scan films.

Since that December morning in 1991, Daniel has undergone numerous surgeries, chemotherapy, and radiation therapy for his astrocytoma. Everything that can be done is being done, including the most advanced forms of laser surgery.

In July 1994, confident that Daniel could receive the same quality of help in Houston, the Furleys moved back to Quail Valley and set up an office for Grace Ministries. They were excited about all the people they could help and were glad to be back among old friends, who welcomed them with open arms.

Then at 5:30 A.M. on August 16, 1994, our sleep was disrupted by a long-distance call from Houston. Cindy Jackson, a nurse and personal friend, spoke words that my sleep-fogged mind couldn't grasp. "Beaver died last night from an asthma attack." It didn't compute. Maybe I was dreaming.

But Cindy insisted it was true. During the past several years, the Furleys had rushed Beaver to the hospital with five other asthma attacks (aggravated by stress). Although Gina had tried to get Beaver to the hospital in time, this time he had suffocated.

Susan and I flew to Houston for the funeral. I was asked to speak, and it was one of the most difficult assignments of my life. For me, the funeral message was compounded by the suddenness of Beaver's death, the amount of suffering the family already had been through, and the dashed dreams of a new ministry that would have provided so much spiritual and psychological healing.

The night before the service we gathered with scores of old friends at the funeral home to say good-bye to Beaver. As I stood by his casket, several people quietly came up and whispered comments like "Explain this one, will you?" or "Why Beaver? Why someone who helped so many?"

I had no answers. I still don't. The next day when I stepped to the lectern at the funeral service, I could only tell them what I did know: that in part, pain is a glimpse of how we can turn tragedy into investment. The first investment I made was to hold on to hope. Beaver was one of my closest friends, and I too needed consolation.

The Benefits of Suffering

Everyone suffers. Each of us can tell a heart-gripping story about painful experiences with unbelievable burdens. Nowhere in the Scriptures are we instructed to stifle our normal, emotional reactions to suffering. When confronted with on-going human tragedies, most Old Testament writers vented their feelings in language that borders on despair.

David cried, "You have rejected us, O God, and burst forth upon us; you have been angry—now restore us! You have shaken the land and torn it open; mend its fractures, for it is quaking. You have shown your people desperate times; you have given us wine that makes us stagger" (Psalm 60:1-3).

But no matter what difficulties we face, ultimately we will be either a victim of the circumstance or a victor. Either we will be under the pile or on top of it. When difficult situations knock us off-balance, like a blinding left hook to the jaw from a prizefighter, eventually we recover our consciousness. Then we have to decide whether we're going to get off the mat. We can choose to lie down for the rest of our lives, or we can choose to work through the normal stages of grief so we can get on to the next phase of life.

Often I've heard counselors say, "Don't waste your sufferings." That's easier said than done. Such statements sound as if suffering is a commodity that can be devalued or that can appreciate. It's like saying, "Since there are many options where you can place your savings, choose wisely whether it's in guaranteed securities or higher-risk investments." When we're in the middle of pain, it's hard to consider suffering as an asset that has growth potential. But that's exactly what it is.

"Why did this happen to me?" we plead as we grieve, desperately searching for a bigger purpose behind the pain. Somehow, when we believe good can come out of our pain, the feelings of pain and despair are reduced. Each of us wants to see a long-term yield from our experiences, to see some silver lining in the storm we are weathering.

That's what this chapter is about. There are at least ten benefits available to those who suffer and choose to be survivors. These benefits are not attempts to short-circuit or deny the depth of pain, nor are they attempts to heal deep wounds with cheap religious clichés. They are real, practical, scriptural nuggets available to those willing to search for truth.

Investment in Christ, Not Answers

Sometimes it's difficult to understand the mind of God, especially when the faithful ones who love him most and follow him faithfully are treated like dirt. Along with Job, we cry out in our personal darkness with words like, "Why do you hide your face and consider me your enemy? Will you torment a windblown leaf? Will you chase after dry chaff?" (Job 13:24-25).

Not only are there no apparent answers, but at times, God

doesn't seem to communicate anything at all. He is silent, and we wonder if he's there. There will always be skeptics who wonder if Christianity is a farce. But, as Ravi Zacharias says, atheism is bankrupt: "Atheistic thinking is just too incoherent to be true, and as a system of thought, it is incapable of dealing with the intellectual and existential rigor that life places before us." There are too many evidences of God's presence for us to deny he's there. So the question for committed Christians is not, Why do bad things happen? but Why do I feel so abandoned in the process?

Perhaps God is silent because we wouldn't understand his answers. Think how difficult your task would be to describe the majesty of the Alps or the brilliance of a late-afternoon rainbow to a blind man. Even if you used the best possible words crafted by pen or voice, you couldn't capture the actual scene your eye beholds.

If God chose to speak audibly and specifically about our situation, we wouldn't understand the full scope of his acts when elevated into the spectrum of time and the circumstances of all people. Therefore, we only receive bits and pieces of God's perspective. Not until eternity will we see the completed puzzle. And only then will we be able to say, "Aha, now I understand."

God chooses to conceal things for his own purpose. James Dobson says,

> If you believe God is obligated to explain Himself to us, you ought to examine the following Scriptures. Solomon wrote in Proverbs 25:2, "It is the glory of God to conceal a matter." Isaiah 45:15 states, "Truly you are a God who hides himself." Deuteronomy 29:29 reads, "The secret things belong to the Lord our God. . . ." Similar language is found in 1 Corinthians 2:16: "For who has known the mind of the Lord that he may instruct him?" Clearly, unless the Lord

chooses to explain Himself to us, which often He does not, His motivation and purposes are beyond the reach of mortal man.

James Dobson, *When God Doesn't Make Sense*[1]

God doesn't reveal his plans, but he does reveal himself. Jesus arrived four days too late to have prevented the death of his good friend Lazarus. Some of the people in the crowd wondered about Jesus' actions: "Could not he who opened the eyes of the blind man have kept this man from dying?" (John 11:37). Each of us asks that same question, "Couldn't he . . . ?" sometime in our life.

Couldn't he have prevented my cancer (or my friend's cancer)?

Couldn't he have prevented that plane crash?

Couldn't he have held back that earthquake?

As Jay Kesler, the president of Taylor University, has often said: "You can't have *God* and *could* in the same sentence." By his very nature and definition, God can do whatever he pleases. Yes, when Lazarus died, Jesus could have arrived four days earlier and prevented it. But he didn't. And because of the experience with Lazarus, Jesus revealed more of himself. Christ is touched deeply by our grief, and he weeps.

In the midst of our suffering, we have a choice to make. Will we frantically try to figure it out and find meaning in some contrived explanation? Or, will we invest our lives in the one who is God, the one who is deeply pained by the sorrows of the human condition?

Dr. Steve Brown of Key Life Radio Network loved his German shepherd, Quincy. When Quincy got hip dysplasia, the only alternative for relief from the pain was to replace the hip sockets. Although Quincy needed that painful operation, Steve agonized. He knew his dog would return home from the vet's office not wanting anything to do with whoever sent him there.

That night as Steve was reading the newspaper, Quincy's cold, wet nose gingerly lifted the bottom of the page. Then he lay his head in Steve's lap. Quincy didn't understand about his operation at the vet's office. He just knew that in the midst of his suffering, he wanted to be close to his master and to feel his touch.

That's the payback when we invest our sufferings in Christ. We draw near to Jesus, who understands, who feels our pain, and who comforts in ways that only those who lay their head in the lap of Christ understand. One day there will be answers. As Paul says, "Now we see but a poor reflection as in a mirror; then we shall see face to face. Now I know in part; then I shall know fully, even as I am fully known" (1 Corinthians 13:12).

Investment in the Priorities of Life

When I was fifteen and my eight-year-old brother, Don, was hit by that cement truck and instantly killed, my personal faith in Christ was embryonic—only several weeks old. I remember my parents talking about the incident with concerned relatives. They wondered if this experience would solidify my commitment to Christ or destroy it. But, like Quincy, I just wanted to be comforted by my new Master.

Tragedy clears the cobwebs from our lives. The majority of people I've talked to who enter full-time Christian work do so because of some personal tragedy. At such times priorities are often rearranged. As a child, I remember hearing the story of why my uncle Carl became a Presbyterian minister. As a young man, he was working in a Missouri field during a rainstorm. Suddenly, a bolt of lightning struck the barbed wire fence he was holding. He was knocked to the ground, but he survived. He figured his life was a gift from God, and he determined to spend the rest of it in service to God and the church out of a sense of gratitude. The same sense of gratitude was true for me. I invested my life in a search for the best way to impact others. I wanted others to hear the same message that turned my life around and gave me the most satisfying answers to life's toughest questions.

The Bible says only two things will remain throughout eternity—people and the Word of God. And these two things need to top every committed Christian's priority list. Not every Christian is called into full-time vocational ministry. But it's critical that we study God's Word and allow the truth of Scripture to touch everyone we contact. Suffering is a wake-up call for us to sort through our priorities and understand what is ultimately important.

Investment in Help Received from Others

When our world caves in and we suffer the loss of a loved one or the loss of a dream, God often bugles a host of friends, who respond with acts of kindness. This is a great reason for being involved in a local church. If the church is functioning as it should, it becomes one large caring family. The believers rally to the support of anyone who falls and provide strength when the victim feels depleted.

Life is terribly difficult to survive without these types of relationships. Dr. Archibald Hart gives more detail: "Relationships provide healing, both spiritual and psychological. Spiritual healing and maturity are fostered by those who encourage and affirm us and by those who tutor us in the ways of God. Psychological healing is aided by the laughter and the tears that all good relationships offer. When you feel bruised and beaten, misunderstood and rejected, a true friend is like an oasis in a parched desert. True friendship means that there is someone beside you who cares."[2]

Many times the people who respond to our needs during a period of suffering are the same ones we have helped on other

185

occasions. Years (or months) before, when we invested our lives in their pain and sorrows, we didn't know that investment would pay dividends on the day of our own trials. This is especially rewarding if it happens within our immediate family.

I have tried to build faith and encouragement into the lives of my two children. From time to time, I put my arm around my children and tell them I understand their struggles. It isn't idle talk. I mean it, and I pray fervently for them.

All parents face times of discouragement and doubt as they try to survive the daily onslaught of life issues. On one occasion, when I was struggling with a difficult situation at work, my daughter asked how I was doing. At first I hesitated to say anything. I've never wanted to dump disturbed thoughts on my children. But sometimes it's beneficial for children to see that Dad and Mom also have struggles. After I shared the source of my concerns, Erica gave me a tender hug and said, "You've always been here for me, Dad. I'm here for you, and I'll be praying for you."

Her encouragement and faith gave me a lift just when I needed it. I accepted her concern and her prayers like ointment on a festering sore. After investing in a source of nurturing and healing, I felt unbelievably fortunate that God provided family members who knew what it meant to reach out and encourage. More than once, each member of my family has been my oasis in the desert.

Investment in Understanding the Consequences of the Fall
Often it's futile to search for immediate answers to why we suffer. We can learn from Scripture why suffering exists in the first place. If you read the book of Genesis, you know that Adam and Eve's disobedience had profound repercussions for them and for the whole world. They deliberately violated God's instructions. As a result, all of humanity and nature

began to unravel, leading ultimately to pain, decay, and death. God told Adam, "Cursed is the ground because of you; through painful toil you will eat of it all the days of your life. It will produce thorns and thistles for you, and you will eat the plants of the field. By the sweat of your brow you will eat your food until you return to the ground, since from it you were taken; for dust you are and to dust you will return" (Genesis 3:17-19).

You and I, the animal kingdom, and the earth with its vegetation and weather patterns, are in bondage to the consequences of sin until Christ returns. Paul said, "For on that day thorns and thistles, sin, death, and decay—the things that overcame the world against its will at God's command—will all disappear, and the world around us will share in the glorious freedom from sin which God's children enjoy" (Romans 8:20-21, TLB).

In other words, suffering is inevitable in a fallen world. I don't know why Beaver Furley died at such a young age or at such a productive time in his life. But I do know that in a fallen world, asthma swells the membranes in the throat, making it impossible to breathe without medical help.

When I lived in Houston, the evening news reported a grocery store holdup where the gunman killed several innocent shoppers who happened to be in the wrong place at the wrong time. As I watched the report, I didn't know that one of the victims was the wife of a local minister. I wasn't able to attend the funeral, but a friend told me the minister stood and said, "We all live in a fallen world where there is murder and destruction. I don't know why my wife's life was cut short, but I do know we all pay a price. None of us escape the ravages of sin."

I found comfort in those thoughts—not in knowing we are victims of a sinful world, but in the knowledge that God hasn't randomly picked people to get hurt. Everyone—Christians or non-Christians, faithful followers or those who have turned their backs on Christianity—lives in an imperfect world.

Many people assume that every time they stub their toe, it has more to do with a sin they committed that morning than the fact they were careless. They search for a sin behind every negative event in their life. On the flip side, they believe if they follow every commandment to the letter of the law, they'll have every prayer answered exactly as they wanted. Neither of these assumptions is valid. God doesn't provide tit for tat. But many people in the Old Testament found this same equation intellectually satisfying. For example, Job's friend Zophar said, "Yet if you devote your heart to him and stretch out your hands to him, if you put away the sin that is in your hand and allow no evil to dwell in your tent, then you will lift up your face without shame; you will stand firm and without fear" (Job 11:13-15).

The Zophars of the world believe God exacts a pound of flesh for every sinful deed.

This philosophy carried over into the New Testament days as well: "As [Jesus] went along, he saw a man blind from birth. His disciples asked him, 'Rabbi, who sinned, this man or his parents, that he was born blind?' 'Neither this man nor his parents sinned,' said Jesus, 'but this happened so that the work of God might be displayed in his life' (John 9:1-3).

The disciples failed to realize the causal link between sin and suffering in a general, but not necessarily specific, sense. Blindness is one of many afflictions in a sinful world, but it doesn't mean that the blind have been singled out because of a serious moral flaw.

Sometimes it appears as if faithfully committed Christians are abandoned. Often in the Bible, God made a promise to a person, then said or did nothing for years, even decades. For instance, God promised Abraham that he'd be a father. But Abraham watched with aching slowness as his wife went through menopause. The child that God promised didn't arrive until Sarah was ninety and Abraham, one hundred. In a fallen world it's anything but joyous to wait, year after year, in silence, for God to act. But believers who are committed to a faithful journey accept this fact. They know that God will move when the time is right and that the agony of delay will be worth every minute.

Investment in the Opportunity to Appreciate the Ordinary

Nathan Chitty, his wife, Sandra, and their three-year-old son, Nathan Jr., were on their way to New Smyrna Beach. Nathan Sr. had a lot on his mind as he headed east along the winding two-lane road. The mortgage company where he worked teetered on the verge of collapse due to rising interest rates and the slowdown of refinancing. Like any husband and father, he thought constantly about how to provide for his family.

On this first day of deer season, a dog jumped a doe, which leaped in front of a westbound van, sending the doe airborne . . . right through the front windshield of the Chittys' Volvo. Suddenly there was blood, entrails, and glass everywhere. Miraculously, Nathan managed to keep their totaled car on his side of the road and pulled to a stop. Their only serious injury was Sandra, whose lung was punctured. She was hospitalized for five days. Little Nathan Jr. didn't even seem to be traumatized.

Several days later Nathan came into my office and recounted the accident that nearly killed all of them. I asked how his job was going. "Somehow," Nathan said, "it's immaterial. We're just enjoying being with each other and taking pleasure in the fact that we can take pleasure."

Ordinary things aren't ordinary to those who are suffering; they are special. Suffering people don't take anything for granted—like special relationships, health, the pleasure of good food, or the artistic expressions of gifted musicians.

When they step outside, they thoroughly enjoy a squirrel scampering up a tree. They sit by a fireplace and listen to the crackle of wood and the hiss of sap. It doesn't take much to bring contentment to those who have narrowly escaped death or know life will be short. Those who invest in the smaller pleasures discover some of the larger dividends.

Investment in Preparation for Further Trials

Sooner or later all of us will have to deal with the role of adversity. Suffering either makes or destroys people. Take, for instance, Franklin D. Roosevelt. In 1921 an attack of polio forever changed his life. Before that period, the political pros considered him a lightweight—talented, but too anxious to ingratiate himself. Alice Roosevelt Longworth, his cousin, called him "a sissy and a mama's boy." As a privileged child, he had been protected from the slings and arrows of life.

Because of his polio, Roosevelt had to give up or overcome his useless parts with the toughened parts that remained. Then he figured out ways to distract others from paying attention to his deformity. He directed their minds toward the things he was saying or doing. He became a superb actor and a focused leader, with enough steel to face the rigors of the presidency. He turned the disadvantage of polio into an investment.

James Dobson calls this the adversity principle:

Biologists have long recognized this concept, which we'll call the adversity principle, at work in the world of plants and animals. As strange as it seems, habitual well-being is not advantageous to a species. An existence without challenge takes its toll on virtually every living thing. Just look at the flabby animals in the zoo, for example. Food is delivered to them every day, and they need do nothing but lie around and yawn. Or consider a tree planted in a rain forest. Because water is readily available, it does not have to extend its root system more than a few feet below the surface. Consequently, it is often poorly anchored and can be toppled by a minor windstorm. But a mesquite tree planted in a hostile and arid land must send its roots down 30 feet or more in search of water. Not even a gale can blow it over. Its unfriendly habitat actually contributes to stability and vigor.

James Dobson, *When God Doesn't Make Sense*[3]

None of us can foresee our future. The longer we live, the more strength we require to survive all we encounter. Only one thing is worse than facing a life-jolting tragedy—and that is facing it without the emotional and spiritual capacity to handle the shock. We don't seek misfortune. But when suffering comes, it will be far less devastating to those who have been buffeted by lesser winds. As Paul said, "We also rejoice in our sufferings, because we know that suffering produces perseverance; perseverance, character; and character, hope" (Romans 5:3-4).

Investment in Time with Fellow Sufferers
If you or someone you know has recently lost a loved one, you know the companionship of fellow sufferers is both good news and bad news. The bad news is, this special club can turn into a pity party. Some enter the dark tunnel of depression and never escape. They want to be around anyone who will empathize with their plight, but over time they can't find the hand that reaches from the other side to help them out of their opaque world.

However, the same fire that melts also purifies. Some have endured great loss and faced excruciating pain. They still have the smell of smoke on them from navigating their particular battle. Their counsel is valuable. They not only have survived, they walk upright with a confident tone in their voice. They have a source of strength that others don't have; many times they are invested in church support groups and continue to help others who are suffering similar battles.

When Paul said, "If one part suffers, every part suffers with it" (1 Corinthians 12:26), he affirmed the goodness about our relationship with each other. We are interconnected. When someone we are close to is in pain, we can't ignore that pain, as if it never happened. That would be denial or self-centeredness. The reverse situation is also true. We can't live in denial that we've been temporarily disabled by our suffering and refuse to seek the help of those who have walked the same path. If we choose denial, then we've committed an act of self-amputation. Chapter 12 of 1 Corinthians describes mutual support and healing, not cutting off or being cut off. A committed Christian will invest time with those who have weathered similar storms.

Several years ago after I finished teaching Sunday school, a man (I'll call him Gerald) who had been a substitute teacher for the class came to speak with me. But our conversation wasn't about teaching. He'd been invited to go skeet shooting, and since he knew I occasionally hunted, he asked to borrow my shotgun.

I was glad to loan Gerald my gun. The following Monday he dropped by my office, and I gave him a few instructions on how to use the old 1894 Winchester twelve-gauge.

"My wife is out of town for a week visiting my daughter's family," he said. "I'm taking advantage of the time to be with the boys."

The next Saturday, about midmorning, the sheriff's department called, saying they had Gerald's body, along with a suicide note that instructed them to call me first. Early that morning, he had driven to an empty shopping center parking lot, then taped a note to the windshield of his car. Then he sat down on a curb and pulled the trigger. I told the sheriff, "That was my gun he used."

The sheriff said, "I know. Gerald said in the note that you were unaware of his intentions."

During the next few days, we tried to understand what drove Gerald to do this. Anyone who commits suicide is in such pain that he or she sees death as the only relief. Gerald was a middle-aged man with several financial setbacks, and he didn't want to face his family with another impending bankruptcy. Instead of investing the time to talk to others who had experienced the same humiliation, Gerald cut himself off from the body of the church. His death left family and friends with a lot of sorrow but also a lot of anger. His death was so unnecessary because help was readily available. The words *if only* kept playing through my mind: *If only* Gerald had asked to go to lunch instead of borrowing my shotgun; *if only* he had invested time to locate someone who could walk with him through his agony; *if only* Gerald could see how valuable his life was to his family and to the body of Christ.

Investment in a Deeper Faith

Major suffering is a watershed event where everyone makes a choice: either to forever resign in despair, or to plow deeper into God and his Word for spiritual truths that substantially satisfy. This spiritual journey can be equated to the typical growth passages of a human being: from infancy to childhood and adolescence, then to adult.

Let's describe this process of spiritual maturation using the imagery of a child who is learning how to swim.

Wading. New believers wade into their faith, normally with complete trust in God—like infants who completely trust their parents. There is the joy of discovering new identity in Christ and finding out that every past mistake and sin is forgotten forever. These new believers are like children, approaching life as full of possibilities. Eagerly taking advantage of every learning opportunity, they work hard to grasp the meaning and the authority of the Scriptures. The initial form of expression for their faith is witnessing to their friends or family. During the wading process, new believers are primarily focused on themselves, asking questions such as, *What am I learning? How should I behave? What does God think of me?*

Swimming. After a while, wading becomes old hat. It's time for larger challenges. Like children who are no longer absorbed with how their legs function or how to relate to adults and siblings, they begin to explore the universe. They experiment with different forms of worship and seek to identify their spiritual gifts, then employ them for the kingdom. They explore various attributes of God and examine major doctrines of the faith. These "swimmers" coax others to jump in the water with them. They want to share their discoveries with everyone who will listen—but they're also beginning to catch glimpses of pain.

Soon they realize that other members of their spiritual body suffer. Some are in emotional or psychological pain. Some hurt socially or relationally, while still others are anxious or humiliated. Especially in late childhood, children realize they can bring comfort to others who are troubled. Spiritual expression now progresses to include caregiving, as well as evangelism, and turns from being merely self-focused to focusing on the church.

Diving. Eventually, good swimmers want to discover what is fifteen, twenty, or even one hundred feet below the surface. Diving takes not only skill and strength, it also means discovering truths only found in the crevices of deep places, where hearts are breaking. No longer is there a search for spiritual gifts; instead, these gifts are employed to the hilt for a struggling world. Life is no longer black and white. There is a whole world of gray where difficult ethical dilemmas leave believers more bewildered than rigidly dogmatic. The mind searches for deeper arguments to understand the philosophical, historical, and scientific wars waged against the faith.

Divers accept the sorrows of a fallen world. As spiritual adults, they devote themselves to calling people to take a swim. As the opportunity arises, they give care. And they are now capable and willing to be used in crisis situations. Spiritual adults talk as long as it takes with either a skeptic or someone bent on suicide. They care for their neighborhood church and also for Christians in foreign lands. They have a global view and a kingdom mentality.

Often, it takes suffering for people to move from wading to swimming to diving. In essence, suffering gives us the opportunity to grow deeper (however, sometimes more quickly than we want!) as a committed Christian. Although the growth process is painful, it can also be rewarding.

Investment in a Future Usefulness

People can endure almost anything if they feel there's some purpose to their trial. Though it's a mistake to immediately link suffering with a perceived "reason," we can be comforted in knowing that God constantly shakes things—for a purpose.

Like the label on the back of salad dressing, "Shake well before using," shaking and usefulness are twin brothers. God doesn't forewarn, he doesn't explain, he just shakes.

God shook Job—he lost everything.

God shook Jonah—the bottom dropped out of his plans.

God shook the apostles—the vibrations didn't stop until they reached heaven.

An unshaken bottle creates a sour sediment like that at the bottom of a wine vat. This was the picture of Moab in Jeremiah 48:11: "Moab has been at rest from youth, like wine left on its dregs, not poured from one jar to another—she has not gone into exile. So she tastes as she did, and her aroma is unchanged." The nation of Moab had become stale, flat, and sour because she was sedimentary, calcified, hardened.

God restores people and nations by shaking them up. Where this shaking leads is known only to God. All we can do is hang on while people watch the Richter scale record the tremors that threaten our world. While the shaking is going on, we take comfort that God's purposes and his kingdom can't be shaken (Hebrews 12:28). We continue to be faithful, knowing that storms will come and storms will go. No one is exempt.

Shaking, then, is a sign of God's involvement in our lives. If things aren't a little turbulent, we may wonder if God is ignoring us. God doesn't shake just for the sake of shaking. There is a reason. The stuff of life is being rearranged, and people are going to be affected. We may not know how, but we know something is going on. We must rest in the knowledge that God takes great delight in drawing us close to himself until our calmness returns and peace is restored.

Investment in a Future Glory

The old saying "He's so heavenly minded, he's no earthly good" could probably be replaced today with "He's so earthly minded, he gives little thought of heaven."

When was the last time you heard a sermon about heaven? Most people are more interested in the returns of their faith that can be cashed today. But in a hundred years (or less), those returns won't matter. All of us will be in eternity, either heaven or hell, depending on whether we have accepted Jesus as our personal Savior or not.

Heaven is a place the apostle John amplifies in his book of Revelation. Though it's impossible to do justice to such a glorious theme, we know suffering motivates us to look in the window. After describing much of the architecture, dimensions, and inhabitants, John wraps up his personal guided tour of heaven by saying, "There will be no more night. They will not need the light of a lamp or the light of the sun, for the Lord God will give them light. And they will reign for ever and ever. The angel said to me, 'These words are trustworthy and true'" (Revelation 22:5-6).

R. C. Sproul's concluding remarks on this passage reveal a view on the other side of the window that staggers the imagination:

> These words are the capstone of John's vision into the secret chambers of heaven. Again he emphasizes the banishment of all darkness. The refulgent glory of God will bathe His people in light forever. Those who are His will receive their full inheritance. They will hear Him say: "Come, My beloved, inherit the kingdom which has been prepared for you from the beginning of time."
>
> It is this promise, a promise certified by the heavenly declaration, "These words are faithful and true" that removes all doubt about our present pain and suffering. It is this promise that verifies the apostolic comparison that the afflictions we endure in this life are not even worthy to be compared with the glory God has stored up for us in heaven. It is this promise that is sealed by divine oath that our suffering is never, never, never in vain.
>
> R. C. Sproul, *Surprised by Suffering*[4]

Our return on this investment is twofold. First, we look at an inheritance no fiction writer could fabricate. Second, it allows us to loosen our grip on the earthly things we consider so important.

The Bottom Line

Without life struggles, few people would stop to consider their true worth in the eyes of a holy God. As much as we would like to skip the suffering and jump immediately to the principles we learn from being in the realm of the afflicted, it's impossible. But once our world has been shaken, we can go through each of these ten investments and realize that a committed Christian receives paybacks the rest of the world knows nothing about. Although these investments don't eliminate the pain and the tears, they wipe out hopelessness and draw us closer to our loving heavenly Father.

THINKING IT THROUGH

1. Why do you think God is sometimes silent when people suffer?

2. What do the following verses say about suffering?

   - Genesis 3:17-19
   - Job 36:15
   - Isaiah 53:3-5
   - John 9:1-3
   - Romans 5:3-4
   - 1 Corinthians 12:26
   - 1 Peter 4:19

3. When you are suffering, what characteristics of a "helper" do you find most helpful?

4. What has been your most difficult experience with suffering? Why?

5. How has suffering changed you? Have your priorities changed in any way? If so, how?

6. What positive thing, if any, has happened because you suffered?

10
Finish Well

*As he [Billy Graham] approaches his last crusades, the
evangelist remains a man of exquisitely undiminished faith.*

LIFE, NOVEMBER 1994

USUALLY I don't mind flying. The statisticians say I have a
greater chance of dying in a car accident than going down in
an airplane. However, there's always one stretch of airspace
that keeps me on edge—the forty-minute flight between Colorado Springs and Denver.

On a typical summer afternoon the thermals that come
over the Rocky Mountains create more excitement than
what used to be an E ticket at Walt Disney World. One day
the plane ride turned us all into white-knuckled fliers. I

cinched my seat belt as tight as I could stand and tried to act cool. Others on the flight held on to each other. One woman hyperventilated and had to be helped by the stewardess. As we approached Denver the air settled slightly, the shrieks of horrified passengers subsided, then we touched down safely.

The pilot reversed the engines, and we arrived at the terminal accompanied by applause from the passengers and even the flight attendants.

In retrospect, I considered the applause. No one clapped when we took off safely; no one celebrated when we survived three or four major air pockets. We didn't even cheer when the wheels touched the runway. But when it was obvious the journey was safely concluded, the ovation occurred. We applauded the ending.

Jesus said, "No one who puts his hand to the plow and looks back is fit for service in the kingdom of God" (Luke 9:62). If people look back, they aren't looking far enough forward. They aren't fully considering the cost of being committed Christians. Although they applaud new beginnings, the entrepreneurial spirit, and are seen in the front lines of new movements, they quickly scatter when words like *persevere, overcome, maintain,* or *stamina* appear. They forget that, in a ball game, half-time statistics are meaningless.

These days, ending well is tougher because we live longer. A century ago the average life span was nearly half of what it is today. But even if people a hundred years ago lived twice as long they still would not have faced the barrage of options and distractions we face today. They didn't have free access to the variety of temptations made possible through the media or the diversions available with modern-day travel. Back then, the family unit was basically intact, with abundant examples for navigating difficult adult passages. But not so today.

Taking Inventory: Where Are You Headed?

Though it's difficult, ending well isn't impossible. If it is truly a high priority for us, we need to take inventory of the following eight characteristics of committed Christians to see if the road we're on will lead to the finish line or the sidelines:

Perseverance

Ray and Anne Ortlund, in their book *Staying Power,* tell about the three time-periods of every project: A Zone, the beginning; B Zone, hitting problems; C Zone, overcoming.

The A Zone is the beginning. It has to do with motivation. Are we energized about the project? Have we counted the cost? Without motivation nothing gets started, and without counting the cost nothing is completed. Jesus said, "Suppose one of you wants [motivation] to build a tower. Will he not first sit down and estimate the cost to see if he has enough money to complete it?" (Luke 14:28). As the analogy continues, Jesus shows how people subject themselves to ridicule when they don't finish what they start.

Sometimes it's difficult to get started, especially if we are perfectionists. We may want to line up all our ducks in a row in an error-free environment. Unfortunately, such an environment doesn't exist. The best way to begin is by telling other people about our plans. We need to put ourselves on the hot seat, where we have to perform because friends will ask how it's going.

However, it's inevitable that problems will arise. The key to success is anticipation. Solomon said, "The prudent see danger and take refuge, but the simple keep going and suffer for it" (Proverbs 27:12). To take refuge doesn't mean to quit. But it does mean that we don't put ourselves in the path of danger. We find the solution to the problem and then act on it. If we can determine the course we'll take when problems arise, then we'll have a greater chance of making it through the B Zone.

The B Zone is the problem stage. If we anticipate there will be rough days, we develop an attitude of patience. We determine to persevere. Although the temptations to quit will be great, half of the battle is *knowing* we can't quit, no matter what happens. The Bible is full of stories regarding those who succumbed to discouragement and others who overcame it. When Pharaoh resisted letting the children of Israel go, Moses found a growing strength to persevere. However, when the Israelites finally arrived in Sinai and began grumbling about their lack of food and water, it was much harder for Moses to be patient.

To get through the B Zone, we have to pray with persistence. We must take on our problems and deal with them one by one, like swatting mosquitoes. Charles Spurgeon said, "By perseverance, the snail reached the Ark." This is also the way most things are accomplished. The world would look different if people didn't get through the B Zone:

> Christopher Columbus would probably have looked to the Western horizon and told his crew, "There doesn't seem to be anything in sight. Let's turn around and go home."
>
> Military campaigns would have ended differently. George Washington, surveying his ragged forces at Valley Forge, would have surrendered. So would Winston Churchill in the early days of 1941. The march of industrial technology would have zigzagged. Thomas Alva Edison, after spending $40,000 to test umpteen hundred possible filaments for an electric light, would have shrugged and said, "I give up. Nobody will ever figure this out."
>
> Most of the heroes of literature would have been far less heroic. Romeo would have said to Juliet, "You're a real neat girl, but I don't think our families are ever going to let us get married. Maybe we should split up." Captain Ahab would have given up whaling and retired to grow petunias in a suburb of New Bedford.

Time, January 28, 1985[1]

Perseverance doesn't mean staying in a rut. A rut doesn't know where it began or where it's going; it's a meaningless constriction. If you realize you were never motivated to be where you are, no one ever encouraged you or affirmed your calling, you're just going through the motions . . . then get out of your rut. Life is hard enough without having to endure the monotony of uninspired, unmotivated repetition.

The C Zone is when dreams turn to reality. When dreams are fulfilled, they may not look exactly like the original dream. This is where yielding control comes in. If everything turned out exactly as we planned, then it would appear God was our errand boy to carry out our orders. But the wonderful surprise is that most of the time the reality is better than what we originally designed! We look back and see God's hand in our affairs, and we're glad we didn't receive exactly what we wanted.

Hope

Hope requires two things. First, we must believe that God is active in the world and, more specifically, in our affairs. God isn't an absentee landlord; rather, he's in control of the ultimate outcome of things. Second, we must believe everything has a purpose. Each of us plays an important role, no matter what our circumstances.

A person with hope can make it through any B Zone, no matter how long or difficult it may be. As Andy, the inmate convicted of a murder he didn't commit, said in the movie *Shawshank Redemption,* "You either get busy living or you get busy dying." Hope is the determining factor. Through hope we constantly look forward to the C Zone, the day when our dreams become reality.

Hope not only keeps you going, it affects you physically. Israeli scientist Shlomo Breznitz says, "Hope—if it is serious, if it is long-term—leads to physiological changes that can improve the body's resistance. In our studies, we have found two hormones—cortisol and prolactin—that are strongly affected by an attitude of hope. While we don't know the precise links, the evidence points to a strong relationship between such neurochemicals and the immune system. . . . People with a strong faith, whether from religious beliefs or just good experience with trust, are the ones who stick it out in the worst circumstances." [2]

Influence

None of us lives in a vacuum. We may think our lives make little impact on others, but that's not the way it works. Those who live as faithful, obedient, committed Christians have great influence on everyone around them. That's why there are so many stories and admonitions in Scripture about the power of influence. Jesus likened us to salt, an influencing ingredient. Paul told the Corinthians not to underestimate the impact a believing wife could have on an unbelieving husband or vice versa (1 Corinthians 7:16). He told the Thessalonians they had become models of faith, not only to the believers throughout Macedonia and Achaia, but everywhere (1 Thessalonians 1:6-8). The writer to the Hebrews said the testimony of the faithful speaks on, even after they are dead (Hebrews 11:4).

Unfortunately the reverse is also true. Solomon's heart was cooled toward the things of God by his many wives. He didn't end as well as his father, David (1 Kings 11:4). David wasn't perfect by any means, and ultimately the prophet Nathan confronted him about his sin with Bathsheba. It had consequences for both his family and the nation of Israel. Or in the New Testament period, consider the influence the chief priests had in stirring up the crowds to release Barabbas instead of Jesus (Mark 15:11).

Numerous times Scripture warns us to be careful what

influences our life: For example, in Psalm 1:1, the psalmist admonishes us not to walk in the counsel of the wicked. In 1 Corinthians 5:11, Paul warns us not to associate with anyone who calls himself a brother but is sexually immoral or greedy.

No one can resist influences forever; eventually we become like the people we are around. Oswald Chambers said much about influence. His thoughts can be summarized in the following four statements:

The people who influence us aren't those who set out to do it. Such people may try to manipulate opinion, but the real influence comes from people who are unconscious of the impact they have on other people.

Influencing people don't apply pressure. They don't attempt to force us into their mold. Instead, they are so attractive that we want to emulate them.

Those who influence us stand unconsciously for the right thing. They don't have to think about it, or debate it—they just do it.

The influence that makes an impact comes from those who have a real, uncontrived, undiluted relationship with God. We can smell the real thing and we want a double order of the same thing.[3]

Chambers could have added one more characteristic: *Those who enter the twilight of their days without the foul odor of compromise, leaving a legacy of doing God's will, are the ultimate beacons.* They may not be the largest light on the horizon, but they are the brightest and most dependable. For those lost at sea, only dependability matters.

Pacing

Committed Christians believe what the Bible says: that it's utter foolishness to believe anything worthwhile is accomplished without God's participation, and that when God participates there is a sense of order, steadiness, and provision beyond our efforts.

The psalmist says, "Unless the Lord builds the house, its builders labor in vain. Unless the Lord watches over the city, the watchmen stand guard in vain. In vain you rise early and stay up late, toiling for food to eat—for he grants sleep to those he loves" (Psalm 127:1-2).

This passage doesn't encourage the carpenter to put down his hammer or throw away his T square. Instead, it says, "Make sure the Lord is behind your plans, then watch him work when you're unable." This kind of thinking is a reality check on the futility of assuming we are responsible for all the good in the world.

When Susan and I were studying Arabic in Amman, Jordan, we met a number of missionaries from different organizations. Naturally, there were some differences of philosophy about how to live out our faith in a foreign environment. All in all, the differences were good-natured—except for those from one mission who felt our zeal didn't begin to match their faith. These missionaries were critical because we weren't willing to go witnessing every weekend, to pass out gospel tracts during every break, or to suffer exhaustion and malnutrition as a badge of our commitment.

If not getting the proper amount of sleep and not eating properly or paying attention to general rules of health and hygiene were the marks of spirituality, then these folks were the genuine article. Unfortunately, many of them spent a good deal of time in bed recovering from their "acts of faithfulness." When I suggested that forty years of a sensibly paced ministry might be more effective than a burst-and-burn mentality for a few short years, they didn't react kindly to my suggestion. Their philosophy was to burn out for Jesus rather than rust out. Never mind Paul's warning not to abuse our bodies and his admonition that our bodies are the temple of the Holy

Spirit (1 Corinthians 6:19). Forget about the fact that Jesus needed time to escape the crowds, to be alone with God and his thoughts. Jesus repeatedly showed the importance of doing normal human things like dining with friends or attending weddings.

Committed Christians see life as a marathon, rather than a sprint. Pacing is the wisdom to understand the importance of the long haul. History overflows with the litter of burned-out, well-intentioned zealots. Sometimes the most spiritual and useful thing people can do is go to the beach and watch the waves for a week or two. The second most spiritual thing they can do is to tell a friend that they aren't impressed with a Day-Timer that has no white space left between assignments.

Avoid Defection

The Bible doesn't overly promote its heroes or hide its villains. Sometimes they are one and the same. The Lord doesn't mince words. He reveals those who are faking their commitment or those who continue to say the right words even though their heart has forsaken their first love: "These people come near to me with their mouth and honor me with their lips, but their hearts are far from me. Their worship of me is made up only of rules taught by men" (Isaiah 29:13).

It's the Judas factor. Unfortunately, many enter into the hall of shame, unable to end well. Paul railed against Demas, who had deserted him "because he loved this world" and Hymenaeus and Alexander, who shipwrecked their faith.

Many ask, What happened? There's not a simple answer. Often it's a combination of several factors. Very few people truly decide they no longer have the desire to believe and want to be free from their contract with the Lord. Most slip-slide away. They haven't escaped the promise of God's guaranteed covenant of adoption into his family because this promise from God was made unilaterally and is guaranteed on the basis of his love—not our ability to maintain our end of the bargain.

The type of defection that prevents believers from ending well can be summarized in two words—*release* and *grab*. There is a temptation to loosen a grip on faith and cool over time from a lack of contact with other Christians who can sharpen our faith. The busyness of our schedule or the pressing obligations of living crowd out time for personal reflection, meditation, and prayer. Some get bored with the faith. They think they have learned everything worthwhile or heard every sermon on any subject.

This release phase is a subtle deception: "See to it, brothers, that none of you has a sinful, unbelieving heart that turns away from the living God. But encourage one another daily, as long as it is called Today, so that none of you may be hardened by sin's deceitfulness" (Hebrews 3:12-13).

Many don't realize they have released anything. They know they are Christians, they have an impeccable theology, but there is a dryness in their bones. To take away the dryness, they look for some excitement, something to spice things up. Now comes the grab phase.

Paul said people drop out because they desire to get rich, and if this desire goes unchecked, it can lead to "many foolish and harmful desires that plunge men into ruin and destruction. For the love of money is a root of all kinds of evil. Some people, eager for money, have wandered from the faith and pierced themselves with many griefs" (1 Timothy 6:9-10). Grabbing for money, what money can buy, or the influence money brings marks one of the quickest signs of defection.

If these people combine the money grab with other characteristics, such as trying to control their own destiny, not having interest in the greater kingdom of God, showing no interest in anyone but themselves, being unwilling to diligently dig into the truths of Scripture, refusing to leave comfort zones, being disinterested in mentoring developing leaders, or constantly boasting of their accomplishments, then they are defectors. Whether conscious or unconscious, they need to seek restoration.

Hazards

Richard Preston's best-seller *The Hot Zone* tells the horrifying true story about several new strains of virus that originate in the same African rain forest as AIDS. Along the Ebola River in Zaire and, more specifically, from the Kitum Cave on Mount Eglon, come a nightmare called *Marburg* or *Ebola Zaire.* These deadly viruses make AIDS look like child's play. When these viruses enter the human body, they reduce the organs to liquid—a bloody meltdown and sure death within seven to fourteen days.

The frightening thing is, these viruses could be transported on any international flight that contains an unknowing victim. Within hours, the contamination could spread to key population centers worldwide. This virus is so toxic and lethal that vials containing infected blood samples are secured in Biosafety Level 4 units. There it can be handled only by authorized experts wearing space suits in government laboratories, such as the United States Army Medical Research Institute of Infectious Diseases (USAMRIID).

A sign on the door of these Level 4 units says, "Caution—Biohazard." Likewise, there are nonbiohazard viruses that can cause an ultimate meltdown in a person's spirituality, hazards that prevent a person from ending well. We may be oblivious to their presence, but if something isn't done, if an antidote isn't applied, there is a strong possibility we will melt down and leave a wake of people wondering what happened.

We all know people who have succumbed to a spiritual virus that sucked the vitality out of them and left them unable to finish their journey with strength. Although an entire book could be written on these hazards, a general list includes things such as boredom, fatigue, sorrow, cynicism, anxiety, sexual liaisons, addictions, anger, jealousy, greed, or marital difficulties. Whenever we feel drawn into these traps, we should visualize in our mind a red neon sign flashing Caution—Spiritual Hazard Area.

As cupbearer to King Artaxerxes of Babylon, Nehemiah was presented with at least four spiritual hazard areas.

First, he was trapped by his circumstances. But his response was to do everything possible in that situation—he prayed. He was concerned about the physical condition of Jerusalem and desperately wanted to return and rebuild the walls. Eventually, Artaxerxes allowed him to return, assuring him safe passage and timber for construction. But not everyone was pleased about Nehemiah's mission to help the Jews. Three trouble-makers (Sanballat, Tobiah, and Geshem) made deliberate attempts to sabotage Nehemiah's mission.

Second, by chapter 6 of Nehemiah, the walls have been rebuilt, with only the gates left to hang in place. Then, just when the end is in sight, the enemy makes one last attempt to derail the Jews' efforts—one last round of spiritual viruses. Sanballat, Tobiah, and Geshem approach Nehemiah with a proposition: "Take a break, join us in the village of Ono." On the surface, the request sounded harmless. Alan Redpath called it the temptation of the world's fellowship. It's a typical tactic of the enemy: Set aside what's important and be seduced by the more alluring offers from the world. Fortunately, Nehemiah saw through their scheme. He realized it was a diversionary virus and refused, even though they persistently dogged him with the same offer four times. Many have not resisted so successfully. They are on target to accomplish the will of God in their lives when appealing offers derail their mission. Then they become so contaminated that they find it extremely difficult to get back on track.

Third, since the diversionary tactic didn't work, the next virus that was planted was slander: "The report is circulating, Nehemiah, that what you really have in mind is a political revolt with the ultimate desire to set yourself up as king" (paraphrased). This was a tough virus to overcome. When we are slandered, we either want to fight back or quit. *Why should we put up with this garbage?* we tell ourselves, and through this reasoning we stop short of accomplishing what God had in mind. Nehemiah wasn't fooled. He considered the source and refused to be agitated by such reports.

Fourth, the enemies of Israel got desperate. Nothing was working. Nehemiah was about to end well. Finally a man comes and pleads for Nehemiah to hide in the temple. He believes that Nehemiah's life is in danger. This seemed like a sensible request. But it's often the subtle offer for security within acceptable religious structures that prevents us from pursuing the real call of God on our lives. Nehemiah was spiritually astute enough to realize that such an offer didn't come from God. It was the virus of intimidation, and if Nehemiah had capitulated, his name would have been discredited and the walls would never have been finished. Jerusalem would never have been secure.

The greatest lesson we can learn from Nehemiah is how to measure every attack, every offer, and every rumor against our life priorities. Without this kind of spiritual maturity it's extremely difficult to end well.

Joy

Eugene Peterson, in his book *A Long Obedience in the Same Direction,* said, "One of the delightful discoveries along the way of Christian discipleship is how much enjoyment there is, how much laughter you hear, how much sheer fun you find."[4]

G. K. Chesterton stated, "Joy, which was the small publicity of the pagan, is the gigantic secret of the Christian."

What are they talking about? The term *ending well* has the feel of drudgery, a grueling, joyless journey. It sounds like all hard work and stoic discipline—something you endure but you don't enjoy.

Psalm 128 paints this picture: "Blessed are all who fear the Lord, who walk in his ways. You will eat the fruit of your labor; blessings and prosperity will be yours" (Psalm 128:1-2). Many nonbelievers don't see Christians as joyful. They point out that Christians seem to be uptight, straight-faced, and that they don't seem to have much fun.

The problem is twofold. What appears to be a "great life" for the world is often nothing more than a constant entertainment binge to overcome the deadness and boredom of their soul. These folks believe that joy is nothing more than a toy, something to play with until the novelty wears off. Then they search to find an experience that will give another shot of adrenaline. On the other hand, Christians can be joyful even if they're going through a severe trial. Joy doesn't mean slapping a happy face on a tribulation and denying that suffering exists. Instead, committed Christians know that sorrow and suffering are real. But they also know the ultimate source of joy: not vacillating circumstances, but a personal relationship with the God who overcomes circumstances.

From beginning to end, the Bible is a textbook about the blessings God provides for those who are part of his family. There is something beautiful, something powerful, something hard to describe that's available to everyone with the end zone of life constantly in mind. Because Christians who want to end well enjoy pleasing their heavenly Father, they are called blessed.

Character

In his book *The Image: A Guide to Pseudo-Events in America,* Daniel Boorstin says, "Two centuries ago when a great man appeared, people looked for God's purpose in him; today we look for his press agent." Boorstin goes on to describe how we have confused big names with the big man. We have created and admired celebrities, yet no longer understand what makes a person great: "The celebrity in the distinctive modern sense could not have existed in any earlier age, or in America before the Graphic Revolution. The celebrity is a person who is known for his well-knownness. . . . He is neither good nor bad, great nor petty. He is the human pseudo-event. He has been fabricated on purpose to satisfy our exaggerated expectations of human greatness."[5]

Throughout most of human history, the truly great characters scorned publicity but sought to be admired for their truly great accomplishments or the strength of their character. To be a celebrity is fleeting. In fact, time is always an adversary and will always destroy the celebrity. Just try to recall any movie or music industry celebrities from twenty-five years ago. Except for a few household names, each one has faded into oblivion. In another hundred years, who will remember today's household names?

Oswald Chambers said it is important to know the difference between disposition (that with which we are all born) and character (what we make out of our disposition). We may not have control over our temperament, and at times it may even be an enemy, sabotaging our efforts of accomplishment. But those who end well, those who have strength of character, will work at overcoming personal weaknesses.

Character isn't about being well known. It's not about having a personally pleasing and publicly advantageous personality. It has nothing to do with isolated acts of goodness or heroics. Anyone can temporarily act noble. Instead, character is about the total trend, the consolidated thoughts of life. Many have fleeting ideas they want to try out in life, but a person of character has core values. What we see in public is what we get in private. People of character are inner directed. They don't test the prevailing winds of moral opinion.

More often than not, people of character are unsung heroes. Quietly, patiently, and consistently, they teach our children, nurse our wounds, patrol our streets, deal honestly in business, are charitable, kind, and keep their word. They seek no reward other than the satisfaction of knowing they live directed and consistent lives. And they do so throughout their lives.

Portrait of a Christian Legacy

Several years ago at a Gathering of Men lunch I met Henning Von Rieben, an elderly gentleman who looked as if he had stepped off the set of *The Sound of Music* or *Schindler's List*. I was impressed by his aristocratic name and the way he carried himself with an air of sophistication and dignity. His heavy German accent added to the overall impression.

I had a hunch Henning could tell many good stories about his background. I was right. From time to time I got him to talk about his early days of growing up in Berlin, where he was born in 1911. His eyes sparkled as they gazed off distantly, revisiting the times and experiences from his memory. Henning could recall amazing details.

His father, a successful lawyer, was hired by AEG, the German counterpart to General Electric. In his father's steps, Henning pursued a serious education. He attended the university in Berlin and Munich, then received a Doctor of Law degree from Erlangen in 1936. While earning his doctorate, Henning also worked in a bank. Times weren't easy, and Germany was caught in the throes of its most devastating depression. Such economic and social upheaval led to thirty-two political parties and, eventually, to the dreaded brown shirts led by Adolph Hitler.

How I wish I could share the unabridged version of his story with you. But time doesn't permit to explain how he reached England and why eventually he was asked to leave, unable to renew his residence permit. He traveled to Holland just in time to hear that the war had started. Already determined not to return to Germany, Henning boarded a ship headed for Mexico, or so he thought. Instead, it stopped in England. Some officials interrogated Henning long enough to watch the ship sail away without him. For the next three years, he was transferred from one internment camp to another.

Henning didn't seem pained by the memory of that experience. In fact, he had a certain delight in recalling, "Vell, you see, I became sort of a camp manager." He made the most of his circumstances. He made sure every prisoner's needs were properly presented to the authorities. I got the impression this was one of many times during his life that he persevered, overcame, and did his best until the end.

In 1946, Henning came to the U.S. to work in New York for a British/Scandinavian metallurgical company. He retired from this corporation in 1978. His first wife died in 1985, and in 1989 he moved with his new wife, Elizabeth, to Winter Park, Florida.

Henning's life had a pronounced trend—to pursue every situation with intellectual curiosity, never to stop growing spiritually even when he had serious questions about the nature of things. World War II was like a mental lobotomy for many, but not for Henning. Eventually through the Order of St. John, formed in A.D. 1090 as a Christian mission to help the sick, he found an outlet for his religious feelings and for his desire to serve others.

Today, Henning is eighty-four, but he has the mind of a thirty-year-old. He has attended every Gathering Bible study we offer. Whenever we organize men to rebuild or refurbish homes, Christian youth ministries, or other social programs, Henning is always the first to sign up. He continues to wrestle with deep thoughts about theology, his faith, and the consequences of government policies.

Henning is ending well. He's not rich or famous, but he has class. He's a noble, faithful, godly example—he's a walking advertisement of committed Christian living to everyone around him. Like Paul, he is pressing on "toward the goal to win the prize for which God has called [him] heavenward in Christ Jesus" (Philippians 3:14).

The Hennings of the world are under no false assumptions about their lives. They don't see a daily commitment to excel in their walk of faith as an attempt to work their way into God's favor. They know they are unconditionally accepted as members of God's family only because of his love and grace. They aren't trying to obtain perfection or to create a standard by which every other Christian is judged. Instead, they love God deeply and are serious about following him. Those who observe them are enticed to do the same.

The Bottom Line

It's not easy to be a committed Christian these days, but that can be said about a lot of things. It's not easy to make money; it's not easy to keep a marriage going; it's not easy to play the violin; it's not easy to overcome the haunting voices of self-doubt. Instead, we must ask the question, Is it worth the pursuit? If so, then we must stay on the course of becoming a committed Christian. We mustn't give up. If we finish the race, one day we will hear, "Well done, good and faithful servant." What a time of joy that will be!

THINKING IT THROUGH

1. Do you know someone who has "ended well"? If so, describe that person's characteristics.

2. What do the following verses say about ending well?

- Psalm 1:1
- Matthew 5:13
- Luke 9:62
- Luke 14:28
- 1 Thessalonians 1:3
- 1 Timothy 6:9-10
- 2 Timothy 4:7-8
- Hebrews 12:1-17

3. Make a list of all the people you influence. What kind of impact are you having on their lives?

4. What hazards of life might keep you from ending well?

5. Are you a faithful follower of Christ? If so, what gives you the greatest joy about being a participant in Christ's kingdom?

6. What does it mean to be a person of character? Do you have these characteristics? Why or why not? If not, ask God this week to help you become a person of character.

NOTES

CHAPTER 1: Yield Control—Without Giving Up

1. George Barna, *The Future of the American Family* (Chicago: Moody Press, 1993), 67–8.
2. Oswald Sanders, *Spiritual Leadership* (Chicago: Moody Press, 1967), 141.
3. Kathy Troccoli and Bill Montivilo, "My Life Is in Your Hands," Reunion Music Publishing. Used by permission.

CHAPTER 2: Focus on the Kingdom

1. Not his real name.
2. Chuck Colson, "The Abolition of Truth," *World*, 19 February 1994, 22–4.
3. Donald Kraybill, *The Upside-Down Kingdom* (Waterloo, Ontario: Herald Press, 1978), 182.
4. Stephen Arterburn and Jack Felton, *Toxic Faith* (Nashville: Oliver Nelson 1991), 73.
5. Don Koch and Shawn Craig, "In Christ Alone," Paragon Music Corporation. Used by permission.

CHAPTER 3: Put Others First in a "Me First" World

1. Material taken from Abraham Lincoln, "The Spiritual Growth of a Public Man," *The Trinity Forum Reading* (winter 1993): 21

Chapter 4: Take Risks

1. Harry Blamires, *The Christian Mind* (Ann Arbor: Servant, 1963), 28–9.

CHAPTER 5: Study Diligently

1. Daniel J. Boorstin, *The Americans: The Colonial Experience* (New York: Vintage Books, 1958), 225.
2. R. C. Sproul, *Essential Truths of the Christian Faith* (Wheaton, Ill.: Tyndale House, 1992), 65.

CHAPTER 6: Mentor Others
1. Used with permission. You can receive the free newsletter "Mentoring Today" by writing Bobb Biehl, Box 952499, Lake Mary, FL 32795.

CHAPTER 7: Live with a Passion
1. David Kiersey and Marilyn Bates, *Please Understand Me* (Del Mar, Calif.: Prometheus Nemesis Books, 1978), 2.

CHAPTER 9: Turn Tragedy into an Investment
1. James Dobson, *When God Doesn't Make Sense* (Wheaton, Ill.: Tyndale House, 1993), 8–9.
2. Archibald Hart, *Fifteen Principles for Achieving Happiness* (Waco, Tex.: Word Publishers, 1988), 150.
3. Dobson, *When God Doesn't Make Sense*, 147.
4. R. C. Sproul, *Surprised by Suffering* (Wheaton, Ill.: Tyndale House, 1989), 174–5.

CHAPTER 10: Finish Well
1. "Hope Sprouts Eternal," *Time*, 28 January 1985, 92.
2. Anne Ortlund and Ray Ortlund, *Staying Power* (Nashville: Oliver Nelson, 1986), 31.
3. Adapted from Oswald Chambers, *The Best from All His Books*, vol. 1, ed. Harry Verploegh (Nashville: Thomas Nelson Publishers, 1987), 176–7.
4. Eugene Peterson, *A Long Obedience in the Same Direction* (Downers Grove, Ill.: InterVarsity Press, 1980), 91.
5. Daniel Boorstin,"Strengthening Spiritual Balance in Lives of Secular Leadership: The Character Dimension of Leadership," *Trinity Forum Readings* 3 (1993), 24.